Praise for
Sam Davidson

D1405146

"Sam Davidson has given us a blueprint to look inward, find our passion, and go out and change the world."

—BETH KANTER, co-author of *The Networked Non-profit: Connecting with Social Media to Drive Change*

"Sam Davidson is the kind of person who can tell you the truth without hurting your feelings. And he's the kind of writer who inspires you to let go of stuff you don't need, be it old dreams or even older T-shirts, in order to make room for what really matters: your passion."

—AMY LYLES WILSON, co-author of *Bless Your Heart: Saving the World One Covered Dish at a Time*

"Sam has an extraordinary ability to make people see the world in a different way."

—TYLER STANTON, author of *Everyday Absurdities: Insights from the World's Most Trivial Man*

"Sam Davidson helps remind us what real success in life means."

—DR. JEFF CORNWALL, co-author of *Bringing Your Business to Life*

"[Sam's] passion leads us to discover our passions and to live well, with meaning."

—BO PROSSER, co-author of *Lessons from the Cloth: 501 One-Minute Motivators for Leaders*

"How can we live passionately when we are still fooled by the myth that 'more is more'? Sam Davidson . . . invites us to free ourselves from oppressive layers of stuff and, in the process, let our lives breathe more fully."

—DR. JIM BARNETTE, co-author of *Homely Joys*

simplify

your life

how to de-clutter & de-stress your way to happiness

simplify

your life

how to de-clutter & de-stress
your way to happiness

Sam Davidson

TURNER

Turner Publishing Company

445 Park Avenue, 9th Floor
New York, NY 10022

200 4th Avenue North, Suite 950
Nashville, TN 37219

www.turnerpublishing.com

Simplify Your Life: How to De-clutter and De-stress Your Way to Happiness

Cover design by Mike Penticost

Library of Congress Cataloging-in-Publication Data

Davidson, Sam, 1980-
 Simplify your life: how to de-clutter and de-stress your way to happiness / Sam
Davidson.
    p. cm.
 ISBN 978-1-59652-820-8
 1. Simplicity. 2. Conduct of life. 3. Happiness. I. Title.
 BJ1496.D39 2011
 158.1--dc22

2011001185

Printed in the United States of America

11 12 13 14 15 16 17 18 — 0 9 8 7 6 5 4 3 2 1

To Lynnette: Thanks for loving me just how I am.

contents

preface

I've spent the better part of the last five years discovering my passion and then living that passion to the fullest, first by turning it into a career, and then by helping others to do the same. In my most recent book, *50 Things Your Life Doesn't Need,* I detailed how getting rid of what doesn't matter will help you focus on what does. Conversely, once you find what means more than anything else, you can let everything else fall to the wayside.

The recession that hit most of the country in 2008 also brought me into contact with people who had lost jobs and were therefore looking for work. A constant and consistent networker, I offered to have coffee with anyone who asked, using it as a chance for conversation and to see whether I could help them on their pathway. Initially, many people were looking to find the same kind of job they were just laid off from, but as I'd look into their eyes across the coffee shop table and ask, "Did you like your job? Were you happy there?" more and more people said the same thing: "No."

The happiest people I know now are those who have left jobs they hated in order to do what they love. Some of it was beyond their control as they left due to financial reasons (their company had no finances from which to keep paying them). Others left of their own accord—like I did from my job many years prior (which you'll read about in detail)—and never looked back.

I soon discovered the name of the game isn't what you do for a living; it's how happy your life is. Work—the thing that we have to do to make money in order to pay for the stuff we want and need—is an inevitable part of life in America. In our economy, you need to earn money to pay for many basic staples like food, clothing, and shelter. You also need to do something productive in order to spend money on discretionary things like vacations, cell phones, and nicer clothes.

But somewhere along the way, whether it was our nation's innate Protestant work ethic or our innate Protestant guilt, we became more and more frustrated with what we were doing for forty hours a week. Maybe it was that our commute became increasingly longer or that we began to see that "loyalty" wasn't as important a word as "politics" in most corporate settings. Whatever it was, more and more people hated their jobs, adding to the stress and unhappiness that filled their lives and minds, even when they weren't in the office.

There has to be an alternative. If the only option for most of us is to suck it up and slave away at a job we hate until we die or get old enough to retire, then the next forty to fifty years look mighty bleak. If our main path to happiness is paved by how we answer the "What do you do for a living?" question, then we have a lonely and depressing path to travel. Instead, we need to find out what truly matters in order to fill our lives with it so we can—maybe for the first time—be truly happy.

The key, then, is to first find what it is that matters. What makes your heart sing? What, when you do it, do you tell others about? What excites you? What makes you want to rearrange your schedule? What do you look forward to? You may have a different answer to each question above. That's fine—in fact, it's a great place to start. Weighing all of your options is a luxury not everyone has, so the more opportunities you have to pursue something that makes you truly happy, the better. But, just the same, a word of warning: being pulled in many different directions, even directions you love, can eventually make you unhappy. There's something to be said for simplicity. That's why this book exists.

"Simplicity" is a word that can be misleading. On one hand, it can demean, used to describe someone's ways that are backwards, out of touch, or even ignorant. Yet at the same time, we love the idea of living a simpler life. We don't want a life that is stupid; we just want a life that is more meaningful, more rewarding, and so much easier to manage. In order to achieve this, then, the first thing you might be motivated to do is get some empty boxes and fill them with stuff your life doesn't need. I warned against this reactionary approach in my previous book. The point isn't just to get rid of things; rather, it's to discover our own value system that continually reminds us of what's most important. Then, once we know what it is we love above all else, everything else can disappear.

Without knowing what it is we're passionate about—our true north, if you will—we'll just keep buying more and more stuff. We'll continue to be distracted by stuff our lives don't need, not because we're bad or confused people, but rather because we have no compass to tell us what's worth buying. Nothing has yet defined for us those things we'll sell everything else to get. We're simply unsure of what we need more of (and therefore, less of, too).

Simplicity works much the same way. It's not about merely living a minimalist lifestyle. It's not about eschewing all technology or fitting our lives into small boxes. Instead, simplicity is about management and balance. It's about being in line with our beliefs and values. It's about prioritization, knowledge, satisfaction, and action. It's about knowing what we want and making sure we never fill our lives with stuff we don't want.

After college, a friend of mine told me she whittled her life down until all of her earthly possessions fit into six boxes. She could easily look and see in one glance everything she owned. I asked her why she wanted to live so lightly, to make sure all of her stuff could fit into her trunk. Her reply was that she was a deeply religious person, and that if she believed God was calling her to move somewhere in order to serve people, she wanted to be ready enough to do so.

The point then, wasn't less stuff; it was less of the wrong stuff. To my friend, her sense of religious calling and conviction was paramount, and anything that stood in the way needed to go, including everything that couldn't fit into six boxes.

A few years later I contacted my friend again to see how life had been and where she had followed God with her six boxes. I thought her life would have been much simpler since she didn't have all of the things that I do in a two-bedroom house. However, the phone call revealed life had been anything but simple. For her, being willing to move where she felt God led her meant things could get complicated. Broken leases, rented moving vans, saying good-bye to friends, being uncertain of how long she'd be in any given place—all of these things ultimately complicated her life. Sure, she had less stuff, but the path that she chose (or chose her, rather) wasn't necessarily simple.

Let this be a helpful warning: less stuff doesn't automatically mean things will be simpler. Neither does discovering what matters. In fact, your heart, your religion, the stars—all of them could be leading you down a very complicated, but fulfilling, pathway. As I'll detail, simplicity doesn't mean things aren't busy. It merely means that you'll always be doing things that matter. For me, if it doesn't fit within a set of tasks or activities that grow my company or allow me to follow my passion, then I don't do it. Things are simple because my direction is nearly singular.

I love the title of this book. I didn't come up with it; all credit and gratitude goes to the publisher for that one. I'm glad this book isn't only about simplicity and getting rid of things. The subtitle of this book is a stark reminder that there's a point to all of our downsizing and reorganizing: happiness.

Happiness is a fast-growing buzzword. For years, books, seminars, and guest speakers have promised it could be found for one low price and in a few hours' time (I'm clearly guilty of this, offering my thoughts on happiness in book form). The problem, however (and where I hope to be different), is that happiness isn't a product that can be picked up at the grocery store and brought home, opened, cooked, served, and digested before bedtime. Rather, happiness is a process, and it may take you your entire life to achieve it.

I said the same thing about passion in my last book, and appropriately so. For me, discovering one's passion is something that takes time—many years, even—and is something that will happen over and over again in one's lifetime. Finding your passion is a journey you live with, full of deep questions and decisions to be wrestled over. It's difficult, even. Perhaps this is why so few people actually find theirs.

So few people are truly happy, too. All of us have moments of excitement, times that we smile brightly and think that things can't get any better. But, in a flash, we're brought back into reality by an event, a harsh word, our day-to-day responsibilities, or anything else that reminds us that maybe things aren't as great as we think they are. Shaken, we become undone and upset, and we wonder whether we'll ever feel so good again. In these situations, we feel like an unfettered boat adrift on a rocky sea. Far from the security of the shoreline, we bob and bounce with each wind and wave, rocking back and forth. We want to brave the storm, but we really want to be tied to our mooring, held tight by happiness and the confidence that comes in knowing who we are and what we want in life. This is true of people who are genuinely happy and know what their passion is. No matter the temporary setbacks or criticism they receive, they remain committed to their purpose. They stay on track to achieving their goals and dreams, no matter what they may be.

I believe these people stay on track toward pursuing their dreams (and are therefore genuinely happy) because they view such a journey as a process, and not as a product. Once they discover and clearly articulate a passion, they begin to refine it. They eliminate anything that doesn't help them on their journey, minimizing distractions and diversions. They don't waste time. They see where they want to be and accumulate resources that help them get there.

They also know that their passion can change. At a minimum, it will get more specific or change in subtle but important ways. They constantly ask themselves the very questions that helped them arrive at their current passion in the first place. They want to make sure they're on the right path at all times. They want to make sure the destination hasn't changed, and if it has, they want to change course to get there. They view passion as a process in order to live a happier life.

Throughout this book, you'll find sets of processes that will help you live a happier, more passionate, more focused life. Doing so will be complicated at times, but ultimately, life will be simpler because you'll have a focused purpose and know what to do to remain true to that purpose no matter what the circumstances may be. You cannot control the circumstances life throws your way, but you can control your reaction to them. Simplicity will not find you; you must find it.

acknowledgments

To everyone who is desperately looking for meaning, purpose, simplicity, and happiness, this book is for you. Thank you for being bold enough to go searching for what truly matters. Because you exist, I strive to help you find what you're looking for.

To my family—all of you—thank you for keeping me sane, grounded, focused, and reminded of what is most important. I especially thank Lindley for showing me that my ultimate legacy is not what I do, but who I become.

Thanks to everyone I've partnered with, both in work and on this book. Stephen Moseley, Matt Cheuvront, Angie Gore, the Team at Turner Publishing—I don't get where I'm going unless you're in the vehicle with me.

Thanks to Bob Bugg for his courageous example of

how to live life and for letting me use his story. Thanks to Adam, too, for remaining a close friend.

And finally, thanks to you, the person holding this book. Without an audience, this might as well be my journal. But knowing that you'll read something I write and change something as a result motivates me to wake up each day and hone my craft so we can all make the world a better place.

introduction

After reading this book, you will not have to live in a hut. You will not be compelled to sell everything you own, stop taking showers, and meditate. In fact, you won't be asked to meditate at all. Meditation is boring.

This is not a book about minimalism. I will not make you get rid of your TV, your liquor cabinet, your My Little Pony collection, or anything else you consider fun (although if you have a My Little Pony collection and you're older than five, I'm not sure how much fun you really are).

Instead, this book will help you discover what matters and help you pack more of it into your life. Because our lives—our homes, minds, and networks of people—are finite, other things will have to go. But the things that need to go are all things that don't matter as much. You won't even miss them.

Simplicity can make you happier. This book will prove it.

simplify your life

1

what is simplicity?

1

what is simplicity?

Down with minimalism

If you've picked up (or were given) this book, it's because you're looking for things to be a bit simpler (or the gift-giver sees you as a very stressed person). Maybe you feel like the world is moving too fast for you. You feel exhausted and tired. There's so much to do and never enough time to do it all. In short, things are hectic. You want the world to stop spinning so you can get off and take a nap.

This past year, I flew more than I did in the previous few years combined. (You'll find a list of all my destinations later in the book.) When I fly, I always know the *what-do-you-do-for-a-living* question will arise from someone sitting next to me, a common cultural exchange that must happen before we take off. Flying is weird that way. We share intimate space (yes, intimate—have you seen how closely they pack passengers on flights nowadays?) for a few hours, and then your aisle mates are gone forever. Random encounters can blossom into something bigger; corporate lore is full of tales of people meeting on planes and in trains who later went on to strike it rich together. I haven't had such luck. I usually find myself next to the guy with too many gadgets or the woman who hates to fly.

As people file into the plane, looking for their seats while hoisting their overpacked carry-on bags into the overhead bins, my seat mate will usually strike up a conversation and ask me what I do for a living. I reply with half of a laugh and a smile and tell them that I write and speak about living a better life. I will sometimes go into detail about the companies I've started, the projects I've been working on, and what I'm writing about at the moment. This past year, every conversation included a discussion about simplicity.

When I tell people I write about simplicity—about getting rid of stuff—they think I'm a minimalist. They believe this for two reasons:

1. Where else is minimalism more prized than in air travel, where everything needs to fit into the small cavern under the seat in front of you, and where you can't take more than three ounces of something on board with you?

2. They also think this because minimalism as a movement has grown rapidly as of late. There have been countless newspaper and magazine articles on the topic, profiling people who have sold their McMansions in the suburbs and traded them in for small lofts in the city. People are refusing to buy groceries until everything in their pantry has been cooked and everything in their fridge has been eaten. This makes sense, of course; most of us have enough food in our homes to last a month, yet we still insist on going to the grocery store every week.

Minimalism, however, is boring. You heard me. Minimalism as a lifestyle for minimalism's sake is flat-out unexciting, uninteresting, and unbelievable.

This, of course, may be the point. When our lives are filled with stuff, they are invariably filled with entertainment, and with it, distraction. Eliminate the distraction, and you'll eliminate the entertainment, too. Owning next to nothing can be very, very bland.

This is why I'm not a minimalist. I like things exciting. I like them busy. But even in that busy excitement, I keep things simple. Everything is manageable, even though it may seem overwhelming. The question I'm asked most often after telling someone about all the projects and companies I'm involved with is "How do you keep track of it all?"

It's easy: I do the things that are worth doing. I do what I enjoy and I enjoy what I do. Not everyone is so lucky.

When you take out the stuff that doesn't matter—the stuff that truly isn't important—it's amazing how simple your life can get, even if it speeds up and gets busy.

This is the beauty of simplicity as I understand it: less of the wrong stuff and more of the right stuff.

Finding the right stuff

The trick, of course, is to figure out what the right stuff and the wrong stuff is. In my most recent book, *50 Things Your Life Doesn't Need*, I help readers find their passion as they eliminate fifty things from their lives. The trick isn't to just find an empty box and fill it with used items to donate to the salvage store. Rather, the point is to find out what it is you are passionate about and to build a life around it. Once you do, everything you own that doesn't help you discover or live your passion can be tossed aside. If you simply set out to find things to get rid of, you'd repeat the same activity each year. Without any real change in personal values or outlook, you're left adrift in a sea of ambiguity. What matters? What should you buy? What should you toss out? It's hard to know how to make the right decision when you have no lighthouse showing you the way.

The same is true of simplicity as it is for passion. By being honest with yourself and homing in on what it is you treasure, what it is you enjoy, and what it is that gives you meaning and purpose, you'll be able to define what the

right things are for you. Consequently, you can then eliminate the wrong things and keep your life much simpler.

The reason our lives are complex and complicated to
begin with is of our own doing. We say yes to too many
things; we try to live up to others' expectations too often;
we're persuaded to buy things we don't need or want; we
work too many hours for too little money at jobs we hate.
All of these things happen because of a false or misguided
sense of obligation. We haven't taken the time to do the
hard work and discover who we are and who we want to
be. Because of that neglect, we continue to add commit-
ments and experiences that don't excite or mean anything
to us. Instantly, it seems, our lives are busy and anything
but simple.

And when our lives are hectic and hurried, we feel
stressed. And when we're stressed, we're not happy. As the
title of this book suggests, simplifying your life will also
reduce your stress and make you happier. A lot happier.

We each get one shot at life. My motto for the better part
of the last five years has been "You have one life. Do something." (I wish I'd come up with this. In all fairness, I saw it on
a T-shirt.) In my opinion, you may as well do what makes you
happy, not out of pure hedonistic pleasure, but because
if this is the one shot you get at living an incredible, re-
markable, and meaningful life, then you may as well have a
great time at it. Working at a job you can't stand and filling
your days with a boring routine all in the hopes that you'll
be able to travel a bit more when you're a senior citizen

seems like a very risky way to live. Instead, do what you love now. Become the kind of person you've always wanted to be now. Clear out the clutter today. De-stress your mind and body immediately.

Keep it simple. Find what you love and get more of it.

Back to the plane rides: the more I talk about what I do and the person next to me in 18B talks about what they do, they eventually ask me how I did it. How I set out on my own and decided to speak, write, and help others live the life they've always wanted. Before I can answer, they sneak in, "Because I could never do it. I'm a lawyer/accountant/ teacher/veterinarian/administrator and to change course now would be so hard. I just don't have what it takes."

And that's when I tell every person they're wrong. Human nature is such that we don't change until we're uncomfortable. Like the frog sitting in a pot on the stove who will be boiled alive if the burner heat is gradually increased, we, too, will stay put unless we have some kind of crisis moment. A routine can lull us into blissful obedience. But if a crisis arises, we're off to the races, and we'll undergo a drastic life change for the better. That same frog will leap out of that pot if the water is boiled rapidly, and we will change course in an instant when faced with an emergency.

Unfortunately, our world is full of things that aim to make things easier, to give us a false sense of comfort and joy so as to not think we need to make a change. We're led to believe that change is hard and inconvenient and therefore ultimately not worth it. We're being boiled alive by our own lives and we don't even realize it. It's time to recognize that life is short and the pressure is on. If we wait for the right signs, the right time, and the right opportunity, we'll find ourselves in very hot water, unable to escape. Instead, we need a crisis moment. There's no use waiting around for one; we may as well create it.

Creating your crisis moment

I was sitting in my office and I gave myself an ultimatum. I couldn't keep doing the same work every day. I wanted a job I loved doing something that used more of my talents and some of my passion. I was tired of answering to so many people, getting up so early, and doing work that was hardly challenging. If something didn't change I'd keep doing this forever, climb a corporate ladder, and earn a lot of money. Though worthwhile goals, they were hardly ones I cared much about.

I wanted to see my wife more, spend more time at home, and enjoy more of my hobbies. I wanted to start running marathons again. I wanted to see my family more often and spend more evenings going on walks through the neighborhood. The decision had already been made in my mind. I needed to voice it to someone else. If I didn't do something now, I'd forever be complacent. I was creating a crisis moment—an opportunity to act and make things forever different. If I didn't create it, things would continue just as they had.

The clock continued to tick over my shoulder as I scrolled through more business e-mails. I knew that my afternoon would consist of a fight with the printer, a boring meeting, and the same kinds of things I had done the previous few hundred days. My leg began to twitch, a sign that my body was egging me on to get up from my chair and take the long walk to my boss's office. It couldn't be any clearer to my heart, mind, and soul, either. I had to quit.

I had too many ideas, too many other passions, and too little time to spare. I told myself, "I can come back and do this job when I'm thirty. I'll give myself the next five years to chase down my dreams, try something new, and really feel alive, challenged, and passionate in my career. But I can't stay here wishing for something better. I need to go out and find it."

I knocked on my boss's door, which he didn't expect. I told him how I'd been feeling. I told him what had been bothering me, that I was appreciative of the opportunity he'd given me over the previous two years, but that it was time to move on. I didn't have a problem with the pay, the company, or the customers. I had a problem with me. The job wasn't a fit, and I couldn't do something for money that didn't excite me or use my passions or talents. I had to move on.

"That's stupid," he said.

He was a lifetime hotel guy. He'd been in the business since before he was my age and would stay a few more years before retiring. He'd done well for himself, still relatively young by business standards. He worked long hours, was away from home every Saturday, and loved every second of it. He'd found a career, a job, and a company he was passionate about. I hadn't. He didn't sense the difference.

"You're good at what you do," he continued. "Why would you leave now? You've been promoted quickly and you do good work. Keep working your tail off and you'll be successful. You have a chance to make a [expletive] ton of money."

I wanted to interject that it wasn't about the money. Unlike him, I had no kids or major expenses. I didn't need all the money I was making. It definitely wasn't making me any happier. In fact, the hours, the workload, and the pressure made things everywhere much more stressful. I didn't care about making a [expletive] ton of money. I cared about being happier.

He kept going: "Look at me. I started in the business when I was twenty. A few more years and I'll be retired. I'll get a part-time job at a hardware store just to have something to do in between visits to see my daughters at college. I'll keep at it a few more years and I'll be set. Then I can spend time doing what I really want to."

"What if you get hit by a bus tomorrow?" I blurted out.

I wanted to take it back. This wasn't a meeting about his career, but mine.

He paused, as if he never thought about the question before. It certainly didn't fit into his plan. Getting hit by a bus would severely hinder what it was he was trying to accomplish in work and in life, and my bringing it up seemed to rattle him a bit. "So be it," he replied. "The point is I'm going to keep working and making a lot of money as long as I can."

Seeing that our discussion was going nowhere, I soon directed the conversation toward putting in my two-week notice, what sort of exit procedures there were, and how I could assist in hiring or training my replacement.

Later that night, I went for a walk around my neighborhood with my wife, a giant grin plastered across my face. I was in the midst of a crisis I'd created, leaving a stable job with no long-term plans. I couldn't have been any happier.

2

why simplicity matters

2

why simplicity matters

A cautionary tale

Four years after the conversation with my hotel boss, I found myself loving what I was doing for a living. The company I started, Cool People Care, was enjoying moderate success. It wasn't profitable, but it was growing nationally. I was called upon often to travel and speak to college students and at nonprofit conferences about volunteerism, online advocacy, and social entrepreneurship. I was proud of what was being accomplished but wasn't sure what was next.

I had articulated my passion: telling stories that need

telling to motivate others to change the things that need changing. But I still wasn't sure what forms it would take. I had published my first book, *New Day Revolution,* had become a trusted voice on pertinent topics, and had gotten to meet many interesting people and organizations. I was happy, but busy. I worked more hours than I did at the hotel. In fact, I woke up earlier than when I had to get up to be at work at the hotel. I now had to arise well before 6 a.m. just to answer e-mails, solve company problems, and continue to grow our online footprint.

When you work for yourself, you get to be your own boss. But sometimes, even that boss is a jerk. If you're working hard and tend to want to make sure things are perfect—like I do—you're easily your worst critic and your hardest taskmaster. Nothing is ever good enough and no job is every truly finished. Second-guessing is rife, as is doubt, fear, and worry.

Happiness—when it comes—often brings an entourage.

Then, one day, everything changed. It seemed like a regular Tuesday for me. I was taking a break from work (my office is in my house) to enjoy a cupcake and catch a sports program I had taped. My wife walked down the stairs to say hello. Then, she spoke those four magical words that can evoke excitement and trepidation in anyone: "I think I'm pregnant."

I had never had anyone say this to me before, so I responded the only way I could think of. "Okay," I said as I continued to devour the cupcake (I did pause the TV). As both of us exchanged glances and nervous smiles, my mind was racing. I was already busy. I loved what I did, but how would being a father impact my work schedule, my career goals, and my big ambitions? How much would a baby cost? Would we make enough money to pay for everything it might need? How much time would it take to be a good dad? Would I sleep even less than I already was?

Question after question kept coming. My wife and I were certainly happy, but would it stay that way? When the initial gleeful glow faded off our faces, what would sustain us? Having a child was clearly a priority for us, but if we were to manage everything and stay happy, things would need to get simpler.

But they didn't, at least not initially. What I've discovered in the last year, however, is that things can stay simple if you can maintain focus and continue to add only things to your life that matter. Let everything else go.

A few months later, I began taking on more projects. In addition to my responsibilities at Cool People Care, I took on what amounted to a full-time job helping a large environmental nonprofit organization design, launch, and promote an online resource for teenagers. I had barely begun the work when the calendar turned 2010, which would be the busiest year of my life.

It's not only about less

One might think that I am the absolute last person Turner Publishing should have found to write a book about simplicity. Any casual observer could look at my 2010 and conclude that all of the activity therein would disqualify me from saying anything about living more simply. Here's a quick look at what I did in 2010.

Became a father. In January, my daughter showed up, forever changing how I think, how I feel, and how I live. I experience everything that a new parent does: lack of sleep, getting sick, worrying like never before, changing more diapers than one can count, going to the pediatrician for any little sniffle. But I also experience extreme elation, unconditional love, and proud satisfaction. My schedule would never be my own again.

Took my company to new heights. After unprecedented flooding hit Nashville, Tennessee, in May of 2010, the We Are Nashville campaign was born. Begun by blogger Patten Fuqua, We Are Nashville became a rallying cry for every citizen in the city as Nashville began to rebuild by lending a helping hand to every neighbor. Cool People Care took on the awesome responsibility of turning the rallying cry into a fundraising tool to help people rebuild their homes and lives. What we thought would be an experiment in designing and selling a few hundred shirts and stickers quickly went viral. After our shirt appeared on Anderson Cooper's CNN show and in every local media outlet thereafter, we proceeded to sell more than 10,000 shirts all over the world. To date we've helped raise over $100,000 for flood relief efforts. Doing so meant even more sleepless nights and lots of customer service headaches.

Traveled more than ever. The places I went in 2010 reads like a life's worth of plane rides and hotel stays. I spent time in Washington D.C., Chicago, Chattanooga, Knoxville, Birmingham, Salt Lake City, Orlando, Buenos Aires, Atlanta, Raleigh, Minneapolis, Denver, Boulder, Dallas, Fort Worth, Baltimore, Waco, Philadelphia, San Francisco, and Athens. Most of this was business related as I was selected to be a finalist in Fairfield Inn and Suites Small Business Challenge, allowing me nearly ninety days to travel and grow my company.

Began new projects. Working directly with nonprofits, I helped many community organizations more effectively reach young people in their work. Whether it was creating Web sites, thinking about effective marketing, or developing a more robust digital presence, I continued to work with organizations doing exciting and meaningful work.

Started another company. As much as I claim not to be a serial entrepreneur, I may be headed down that pathway. In late 2010, I began Proof Branding with colleague Matt Cheuvront. We saw a need to help organizations and companies better brand themselves online and off.

Wrote a book. In December of 2010, *50 Things Your Life Doesn't Need* was published by Turner Publishing. I spent the better part of the year writing it, and once it was ready to be released, I put countless hours into promoting it online via social media, traditional media, and blog posts. The hard work paid off, and now lots of people have figured out what their lives don't need, as well as what their lives' true passions are.

By all means, I did a lot in 2010. People often ask how I manage so much busyness, and I reply with, "My schedule is never consistent, but usually flexible." I rely on online calendar tools and a smart phone to keep myself in sync. But even with all this busyness, travel, and taking on new challenges, I was always happy. I managed to get it all done. Simplicity, I feel, isn't necessarily about doing less—it's about doing less of the wrong thing. If something doesn't matter, if you don't enjoy it, or if it's not worth doing, then by participating in it, you're increasing the work and hassle in your life. If you want to be happier and live more simply, then you have to do less of the wrong things and more of the right things.

Deciding what is right and what is wrong is what the rest of this book is about.

3

simplicity is a process

3

simplicity is a process

If you ask most people, they'll tell you that their New Year's resolution or a major goal is to live more lightly; they usually want to lose weight or clear out the clutter from their lives. Most of them will want to do either worthy pursuit in order to be happier. At the end of the day, we all want to go to sleep with a smile on our faces, content with and even elated at the way life is going.

The point of simplicity, then—as this book's subtitle suggests—is to be happier. If we're chasing simplicity for simplicity's sake, we'll arrive only at minimalism, and that, as you recall, is boring and even pointless. Instead, we can live simpler lives by doing what makes us happy. Finding that usually comes by living out our dreams (your own of which you will articulate in an upcoming chapter). It also comes when what we do matters.

Finding work that matters is easier said than done. We all have to work for a living if we want to earn money to pay for the things we want and to support the people we love. Very quickly, then, we're faced with a crisis when it comes to doing what makes us happy.

The crisis of work

When we finish college and get out into the real world, a very real crisis hits: the crisis of work. This—and not the fact that they're simply notorious slackers—is why your twenty-something son or your boss's daughter feels entitled to quit their job and travel the world. For the first time, they're faced with reality: a lifetime of work, doing the same thing forever in order to live a life they don't really want to live.

Their—and our—natural instinct is to run. To quit work, pack it up, and live a life we've always imagined. Shirk responsibility, buy a one-way ticket to Rome or Los Angeles, and see what happens. It's not necessarily noble, but it's a gut reaction when faced with the crisis of work. This is also why it seems so many people want to start their own business, spend a year volunteering, or try to write a book. Each of those things seems like it's not work. Each of those endeavors might free someone from the day-in, day-out doldrums that everyday life creates.

Work is a crisis for new graduates—and for anyone—
because you're forced to face the reality that this is it. This
is what you're about to spend the rest of your life doing.
You will work this job for forty hours a week for the next
forty years until you're old or sick, and then you can try
to enjoy life. No wonder so many people experience the
fictional terms of a "midlife crisis" and "quarter-life crisis."

I think those terms are made up based on the wrong
data. Midlife and quarter-life crises happen to people
around ages twenty-five and fifty, but aging is not what
causes them; work does. At twenty-five, you're faced for
the first time with long-term prospects. Up until then, you
only had to think about life in four-year increments. Pri-
mary school, middle school, high school, college—each
was four (or five) years long. You knew that even if you
didn't like something, your circumstances would automatically change soon enough. There was a finish line (gradu-
ation or promotion) just around the corner.

But when an actual job enters the picture, things are
different. There are no automatic promotions. Bosses aren't
like professors or little-league coaches. There is no party
in four years, no best friends to be made. What's a new
employee to do?

Likewise, around fifty, retirement looms. It's not immediate, but you can see it. It's also the age at which you're
likely to be replaced with a younger model at work, depending upon what you do. You start to look at life and
realize you've spend the last twenty-five years building a

career and neglecting what really matters. Your kids are older and getting ready to leave home (or are already gone). You'll be reconnecting with your spouse on a level you haven't experienced in years. Do you even know what you truly love doing since so much of your time has been occupied by work? Are you ready to get back all the free time you kept denying yourself so that you could earn a few more dollars?

Alas, in a capitalistic world, we're defined more by what we do to earn money than by the kind of people we want to be. Titles like "Regional Manager," "Division Vice President," and "Sales Rep" signal more to people than qualities like "ambitious," "kind-hearted," or "great friend" do. Wouldn't life be simpler if we didn't have to work so hard to earn so little money and a title, and instead we were free to live as the kind of people we are when we're at our best? What if we could be known by our ideal selves instead of what our business cards say?

Of course, life would be simpler if we had no jobs at all, but that's not realistic. What is possible, however, is to not look at our work as a crisis point or even a defining characteristic in our lives. Instead, we need to view work as a vehicle, not a destination. Work—for many of us—is something we have to do. Very few people work at their dream jobs, and those who do usually created an opportunity for themselves to make that happen. So, unless you're willing to take the financial and legal risk to start something from scratch, you're looking at a lifetime of working for someone else. This is manageable if you look at it the right way.

In order to simplify your life and stay sane, here are three tips for avoiding the crisis that work creates, making sure that you stay employed and stay happy.

1. *Tell yourself: Work is not the most important thing in life.*

It's awfully tempting—when so many people put so much stock in a job title—to fall into the pattern and temptation of prioritizing work more than anything else. Perhaps by now you've heard the story that no one on his deathbed has ever uttered the phrase, "I wish I'd spent more time at work." When faced with death, people immediately think of loved ones—family and friends—and not deadlines or business deals.

This is why it's important to always keep your dreams in mind. Making sure those stay central when making decisions will help you remember what makes you happiest. You never want to be seen as irresponsible or selfish, but you do want to know what decision to make in any given circumstance. It's okay to take off work and use a vacation day when your daughter has a starring role (or any role) in the school play. Being a parent or a great friend should take higher priority than being an obedient worker.

I'm reminded of a personal story from a friend's dad. When looking for an administrative assistant for his new law firm, he asked his adult daughter if she'd like the job. She was a very successful retail manager and was doing well for herself, climbing the corporate ladder at a national company. She and her husband recently had a baby, and her priorities (rightfully so) shifted. His offer?

> I offered her a deal she couldn't refuse. Come to work for me and I will pay you substantially less money than you are making but I will recognize that this job is not the priority of your life. She accepted my offer (after all, I am a professor of negotiation), and it has worked out wonderfully for me. I have been true to my word— she has been drastically underpaid.

Bob's offer to Jenny was the right one. The work wasn't overly challenging or invigorating, but work wasn't the most important thing in her life anymore; her son was. In order to keep her son her first priority, she avoided the crisis of work by recognizing it didn't mean as much. Instead of defining her life by how quickly she could climb the ladder and how much money she could make, she instead decided to take a job that allowed her to keep the main thing the main thing.

2. *Your work can be made more meaningful when you can match a talent with a passion.*

It's important to know what you're good at, and what

you like doing. You can avoid the crisis of work if you find work you love or work you can excel at. Many young people face the crisis of work because they are forced to take a job they hate or can't do well. Saddled with student loans and needing to pay rent, they take sales jobs when they can't handle the workload or don't have the skill set that's needed. They decide to work in hospitality but don't have a passion or a talent for customer service. Work can get unbearable very quickly when you're doing something you're unqualified for or don't enjoy.

The key is to first figure out your passions, which you will do later in this book. Once you've done that, you can begin to look for a job that provides a service or product in line with that passion. This is most easily found in the charitable world. If you're passionate about literacy or adoption or ending homelessness, then you can be fulfilled and happy at a job working for an organization that focuses on those things. Whether you're running the nonprofit as executive director or helping answer the phones and clean the toilets, you can go home happy knowing that you're working on something you love each and every day.

Or, you can find a job that you're good at doing. Whether you're a whiz at numbers or a marketing genius, being successful and recognized for your hard work can also do wonders for your corporate soul. It feels good—and work can be fun—when you continue to hit your numbers, get promoted, and have accolades heaped upon you by higher-ups. Once you have identified your talents (or strengths, as we'll call them in a future chapter when you begin to write your Personal Strategic Plan), applying to jobs that utilize them could help you avoid the crisis of work. You won't feel like hating your eight hours a day when you're the best at it.

However, it is important to note that neither of these will sustain your happiness and the avoidance of the crisis of work for long. Passions change, and continually excelling at something over and over again could get boring. Although finding work you do well or that excites you is a great start, it is not the end. The ultimate goal is to find work you love and that you do well.

I was chatting with an old friend during the Thanksgiving holiday one fall. It was the Saturday afterward, and a group of us who were close friends in high school decided to get together for a meal and catch up. Facebook makes it easy to see pictures and learn about an old friend's life one status update at a time, but sharing a drink and a laugh does much more for one's soul than any of our digital tools can provide. As we all told stories of where we'd been in our years since graduating, Rebecca told me she was unsatisfied with her job.

"I hate work," she lamented as she reached for the salt and pepper.

"Why?" I asked.

"It's boring. I mean, it's accounting work, which I'm great at. I did very well in my master's program and have a job that looks great on paper. I am continually recognized at company functions and I've been promoted twice. The money is great. But something's missing."

"What's missing? A company car? A share of a private jet?" I joked as I took a bite of my burger.

"No," she continued after taking a sip. "It's not meaningful to me. I'm actually starting to hate working with numbers. I'm good at it, but I don't like it. I want to come home at the end of the day and feel like I made a positive impact in some way. Maybe I'll work at a nonprofit."

This piqued my interest since I'd been working with nonprofits in a variety of ways since starting Cool People Care. "And why is that?"

"I feel like I'll be more satisfied if I do work that directly helps people, instead of balancing the books and auditing some huge company."

"And what would you want to do at a nonprofit?" I asked as the waitress brought refills for the table. "There are lots of options depending upon the organization."

"I don't know," she replied. "Maybe accounting?"

I halfway laughed. I then explained that if she hated working with numbers, she'd probably hate working with them even more when they were much smaller than what she was used to auditing companies on Wall Street and Madison Avenue. Instead, I challenged her to think about work that motivated her, as it sounded like making a difference was very important to her. Then, while her accounting program could get her in the door, I also reminded her that she didn't need to stay in that position once hired at a charity. She could find another opportunity to use her talents to make a difference. Then she'd find that sweet spot where she could match a passion and a talent.

This is also possible in the for-profit sector. Whether you're passionate about music, sports, art, or technology, you can find a company that matches these interests with your skill set. Once you finish the upcoming section about developing a Personal Strategic Plan, you will have made a list of your strengths. Pair that with your list of passions. Before you apply for another job, make sure the position offers you something from each of these lists. Then, you'll be happier at work, avoiding the stress that comes with the crisis of work.

3. *Your next job doesn't have to be your dream job, but it should get you closer to your dream job.*

Speaking of applying for jobs, especially if you feel like you currently have one that seems more like a crisis than a paradise, know that you don't need to find your dream job now. Whether you are twenty-five or seventy-five, your dream job is out there, and like dating, you simply need to see what's available to know what you like. Most of us may have an idea of our dream job, but it could be very unrealistic. My dream job is to own a major-league baseball team. The last time I checked Monster.com, there were no such openings. As a result, I now have a list of dream jobs, instead of just one.

We can often idealize dream jobs too much. As I've mentioned, most of the people I know who can honestly say they are working at their dream job have created the opportunity and were willing to become an entrepreneur. Others, however, have found their ideal work opportunity by finding a place that matched a passion with a talent. Many others, unfortunately, are still looking, claiming to be holding out until it magically appears.

I realized this during a recent conversation with a friend. Kat was hoping to find her dream job in San Francisco and be able to leave her boring position on the other side of the country. She applied for job after job, many of which she was underqualified for. Also, during the recent economic downturn, when some hiring managers have been receiving as many as 100 applications for every open position, it would be tough for Kat to stand out from the crowd without being nearby.

I asked her what was more important right now: the job, or the location? Was it more important that she live in San Francisco or that she find a job she loved doing? Based on that answer, she'd need to expand her search, either into other cities or other sectors in California. I also helped her to realize that she didn't need to find her most ideal job offer right now. She was twenty-six. She could wait a few years before finding her dream job, especially since her notion of that could change in the next few years, like if she started a family (remember Jenny from the earlier example?).

Instead, I let her know that the next job didn't need to be her dream job, but it did need to get her closer to it, whether it meant working in the same industry or the same city. Staying where she was isn't an option as it got her neither. She needed upward movement, a clear trajectory of progress. And so do you, if you want to avoid the crisis of work. Be looking for and moving toward your dream job. Finding it happens one step at a time, not with a giant flying leap.

The crisis of death

Along with work, death can present a major crisis in our lives. If you're simply waiting for a crisis to arrive, you may never recognize it. By highlighting work and death as two major crises, I hope to help prime you to take the necessary steps to simplify your life and do what you've always dreamed of.

Work can be a wake-up call when we realize that doing the same thing for the rest of our lives can be meaningless and stressful. Likewise, death, which will find us all eventually, can make us wake up and realize that the time to do something with our one wild and precious life is now.

This can easily be realized each time we go to a funeral or when a young person's life is tragically cut short. While working at the hotel, one of my first employees died unexpectedly. One day he was helping install sound equipment. He didn't show up the next day. I later found out that he was hit by a car while driving home on his motorcycle. The unexpected nature of his untimely passing forced me to take stock of what I was doing with each of my days on the earth.

I was further reminded of this when reading about the odd occurrence of the death of a woman in France. She was scheduled to be on a flight from Brazil to Paris that crashed shortly after takeoff, killing everyone on board. Because of a series of events, she missed her flight. A later one took her safely home. Two months later, however, she was killed when a bus hit her as she was riding her bicycle. Life is fair: death eventually gets us all.

Death is a crisis because it's so finite. It's terminal. It's the end. As such, we face extreme pressure and stress to get done what we need to get done before death hits. The tricky part, of course, is death's uncertainty. With work, we know that it ends each day at 5 p.m., or after forty years. Death, on the other hand, strikes at any time, no matter how complete our plans are. Just as my hotel boss thought he'd have plenty of time to work hard and then play hard, fate could easily take his best-laid plans and make them irrelevant.

This is the problem with the "Deferred Life Plan" as coined by Randy Komisar in *The Monk and the Riddle*. The plan is that first, you do what you have to do in order to earn money. Then, you can do what you want to do. Deferring life until we've made enough money or done enough stuff is foolish, not just because of death's uncertain appearance, but also because waiting to truly live until we have "enough" money can be a fool's game. We'll certainly think it's okay to keep chasing the dollars or the fame because one day, eventually, we'll have enough. But it rarely works like this, mainly because we rarely take the time to define "enough." We never know, then, when we've found it because we don't know what it looks like.

Death, of course, means we can accomplish no more. Working a job we hate just to earn money or notoriety might seem like a path that leads to fulfillment, but chasing milestone after milestone for their own sake will never help us figure out what we really want to do. Chasing achievements may seem like a great game plan, but when we die, we're unable to play any more. Game over. We're going after products when what we need to integrate into our lives is a process. Instead of asking, "What have I accomplished today?" we should ask, "Who have I become today?"

Being should always take priority over *doing*. *Becoming* is more important than *owning*. Simply accumulating stuff and titles makes our lives cluttered. Focusing on becoming the right person is a better bet as it will simplify our lives and help us to remember what truly matters. Best of all, by living in a way that helps us become our best selves, we'll avoid the crisis of death. Come when it may, we'll rest assured knowing we are becoming who we should be. We'll never have enough money or power, but we can make substantial progress toward who we want to be. The crisis of death (and the accompanying stress) can be removed and our lives made simpler by focusing more on the process of becoming who we should be rather than on the product of what we can earn in a lifetime.

Beginning the process

Therefore, in order to work around these two crises—work and death—and to figure out what matters, you need to undergo a constant personal process, complete with two key tools. The first tool, the Dream to Action Plan, will help you define your dreams and passions and bring them to reality. Doing so may help you avoid the crisis of work by focusing on what's more important: matching a job with a passion or talent, or getting you closer to your dream job.

The second tool is your Personal Strategic Plan. This will allow you to keep your life free from clutter and stay consistent in order to live a simpler life. Without either tool, your life will continue to remain stressful as you spend too much time doing work you rarely enjoy. It will also mean that you'll have no process in place to keep things simple over the course of your lifetime. Spending time to develop these tools in your own life is the fastest and most direct pathway toward living a life that is simple and makes you happier.

4

going from passion
to action

4

going from passion to action

Start at the beginning

Lewis Carroll, author of *Alice's Adventures in Wonderland*, has the Queen of Hearts offer Alice this advice: "Start at the beginning, go through to the end, and then stop." I like advice like this: practical, straightforward, and easy to follow.

For the rest of this book, I'll be offering steps, lists, processes, and procedures to live a simpler life. I'll help you figure out what matters in your life and how to get more of it. To do that, you'll need to start at the beginning each time and go until you find the end. Stopping in the middle won't give you the complete results you need to live a life of simplicity. Keep going through to the end, and then stop.

To find what matters, we need to tap into our passions and then act on them. A lot has been written and said about passion over the years (including my previous book), much of it romanticizing that spending fifteen minutes thinking about what makes you happy will magically make you find a job you love. I hate to burst your bubble, but that works only in Wonderland.

Instead, we need a process to bring our passion into reality. This chapter shows you how to do that and includes my personal story on how I did it. Before I quit my job at the hotel, I drove to work in the dark each morning and plotted how I could leave my job. I was thinking on and developing my big dreams—my big plans for a better life for my family and better work for myself. I was driving to a hotel, but really, I was hoping that I was headed toward a better future.

As I mentioned in *50 Things Your Life Doesn't Need*, my passion is "to tell stories that need telling in order to motivate others to change the things that need changing." Arriving at this passion took nearly four years, and even since discovering my passion and looking for relevant ways to live it, I'm always asking myself how I might refine and modify it in order to be happy.

In order to live out my passion of telling stories that need telling so that others may change the things that need changing, I began a company that published articles and interviews highlighting how volunteering and helping one's community can make the world a better place. I'm still involved with that, but I also now write books about how people can discover their passion in life (another kind of story that needs telling). I also speak and lead workshops about these topics. This has all happened in just a few short years. Who knows how I'll be telling stories one day? And, if all this can happen in a relatively short amount of time, I'm fully open to the idea that a new passion could develop at some point and send me down a brand-new path. That's why finding and living your passion in order to be happy is a process; it's always changing.

In fact, I didn't just discover my passion for telling stories within this past decade. It's something that began much earlier. I was seventeen. Or maybe I had already turned eighteen. I just remember that I could drive, was trying to figure out where to go to college, and was very curious to answer that often-haunting question, "What am I going to do with my life?" When you're in your final years of high school, the first question that any relative, teacher, or coach asks is where you're headed to college. I had stacks of brochures in my room and was trying to decide whether majoring in creative writing was a good career decision, whether I could wait to study religion until I went to seminary, or most important, how far the perfect distance was to be from home.

At this point in my life, I felt compelled to be a minister. I was very involved in my church youth programs and enjoyed it very much. Thus, to me at eighteen years old, it seemed like the best career move was to find a college I was interested in, get ready for religious studies in graduate school, and then find a church to work in until retirement. That was the plan, at least.

I did feel a supernatural, religious calling to do this, that something bigger than me was motivating and encouraging me to pursue this line of work. There was both a comforting and exciting feeling to believing that I was "supposed" to go to college, study whatever it was that would get me admitted to a seminary where I could get a master's degree and then become a pastor in a church, preparing sermons every Sunday, eating dinner at church every Wednesday, and making trips to the hospital as needed. That, in fact, was the journey I set out on when beginning college. But it's now twelve years later, and I don't work in a church. What happened?

Quite simply, I went beyond my calling to find my true passion. That process led me out of wanting to work at a church full time and toward wanting to become an entrepreneur. Granted, I could still wind up working in a church one day, but not now. My sense of passion is too great, and the process that forces me to continually define it is decidedly not pointing me in that direction.

After getting a handle on what your big dreams are, you'll begin to focus in on how those dreams might take shape for you, which is the point of developing this first critical tool, the Dream to Action Plan.

Step One: Dream

Robert K. Greenleaf, the guru of servant leadership, writes, "Not much happens without a dream. And for something great to happen, there must be a great dream. Behind every great achievement is a dreamer of great dreams. Much more than a dreamer is required to bring it to reality, but the dream must be there first" *(Servant Leadership: A Journey into the Nature of Legitimate Power and Greatness,* 30).

Dreams. Martin Luther King, Jr., had one. I bet you have one, too. You may have several. They are very powerful things, and when you have one, do not let it go until you've chased it down and refined it into a passion. A dream, as Greenleaf points out, is where it all starts.

Dreams are big and bold. In fact, there is no such thing as a small dream. A small dream is simply a task. If you dream of going to the grocery store, then let's face it, achieving your dreams doesn't take much more than a gallon of gas and a few right turns. Dreams were meant to be huge, outrageous, and audacious. It was a dream that put a man on the moon. It was a dream that allowed Google to organize all the world's information, and a dream that motivated the Wright Brothers to get their flying contraption off the ground.

A dream is the first part. It's the seed you plant from which you hope to grow big-time results. Dreams are supposed to be gigantic, and therefore vague. Dreams get you started. They set you down a pathway that gets narrower as you begin to act on those dreams, but being broad and expansive are great characteristics for dreams. The bolder, the better.

What are your dreams? What do you think about when you think about nothing at all? What do you hope to see in the world one day? What do you think needs to be created? How can you leave a mark on this planet? What can you do to make a difference? What's your big, ambitious goal for your life and the life of those you know and love?

Do you dream of inventing a better type of battery? Would you like to see safer schools? Do you want more options when it comes to our political system? All of these dreams are worthy; each is ambitious and broad. A lot will be needed to bring these dreams into reality, but these are great starting points.

If you've never taken time to dream, it's a routine that's worth adding to your schedule. This book is about eliminating and simplifying things, of course, so in order to fit this new activity into your life, make sure to put it in place of something you do that is not adding as much value. Skip a TV rerun once a week and make a list of your dreams instead. Dream (like I did) while driving into work. Eat lunch every Monday with a pen and journal and write down any dream that comes to mind.

As you do that, here are six questions to ask yourself to get your dreaming ideas flowing. Reviewing these questions as you dream will help you stay on task while eventually being able to articulate your dream so you can share it with others who will support you and help you further refine it.

Question #1: What do I like doing?

Let's start simple. What do you enjoy doing? What are your hobbies and interests? What brings you joy when you get to do it? Write down as much as you think of. Include even the things that don't seem so lofty, like participating in your bowling league or keeping up with celebrity gossip. I highly doubt these will make it to the final list when you try to turn dreams into realities, but remember: you're starting broad and general and big. List all of your interests and personal pursuits. What do you do in your free time? What do you look forward to doing after work or on the weekends? You might have the beginning of a dream, so don't ignore anything that brings you a bit of happiness.

Question #2: What makes me angry?

While seemingly negative, this question is very insightful. The things that anger you could be the very things that motivate you to eventually take action. Rosa Parks, Susan B. Anthony, and Harriet Tubman were all angered by something that motivated them to act. As a result, our world is forever different. You don't want to dwell on your anger, but you do want to use it as a catalyst for movement. Listing things you can't stand and that infuriate you may allow you to uncover a big dream for yourself.

Question #3: What needs changing?

Building upon the previous question, what do you see in the world that needs to be different? If you've ever said, "There oughta be a law . . ." what were you referencing? Take a look around your community. What should be different than it is? Is there a way that a business process at your company could be modified? Is there a better or easier way to get through your daily routine? What could be done faster, simpler, or produce more results? Seeing how things could be and articulating a better pathway could form the core of a great dream.

Question #4: Who needs help?

Who in your neighborhood could use help? Where have you recently spent time volunteering? Your dream doesn't have to be directly related to some altruistic or philanthropic purpose, but it could be a great arena in which to explore a dream. Blake Mycoskie, founder of the wildly popular TOMS shoe brand, saw a need to provide kids with shoes in developing countries. As a result, he chased down his entrepreneurial dreams and began a company that donates a pair of shoes to a child for every pair purchased. You never know where a dream to meet a need can blossom into a new life for yourself and your family.

Question #5: What am I good at?

Don't ignore your talents. Ever. And don't feel selfish

or prideful about writing them down. Identifying what you do well will come in handy when you create your Personal Strategic Plan, which I detail in an upcoming chapter. It will also call your attention to something you can build a dream around. If you're already great at something, it's easier to make your dream come true. I might dream of playing poker professionally, but I'm no good at telling when someone is bluffing. Chasing down that dream would require a lot more work on my part than, say, writing a book or starting a business. Each of those are things I can do well. As a result, those dreams can come to fruition in a much more expedient fashion.

Question #6: What could be?

George Bernard Shaw first penned the famous line, "You see things; and you say, 'Why?' But I dream things that never were; and I say, 'Why not?'" (later attributed to Robert Kennedy). The question posed is a great one: what could be and why couldn't it be so? This question should really allow you to dream big. There are no limits to this question—anything is possible! What would you like to see happen differently? What would you want to see invented or created? If you can think of it, write it down. It doesn't matter how outrageous or outlandish your answer to this question is; we'll refine it a bit more when we get to the next steps.

Step Two: Find your passion

Once you've spent regular time dreaming and have a lengthy list of dreams, it's time to begin to narrow things down by focusing on a passion. A passion is something that can be summed up in one sentence and comprises your life's work—at least for a season.

A passion is more specific than a dream. Whereas your dreams are big, bold, and audacious, a passion is more defined. A passion may take into account a place or a population—where you want to do what you want to do and with whom you want to do it. A passion also is more personal. It's what drives you and motivates you; it's why you wake up early and stay up late to bring your dream to light. Your passion is what excites and ignites you. Other people can see your passion, whereas only you can see your dreams.

To begin to better define your passion, ask yourself the following six questions. As you answer them, see how they align with any of the dreams you wrote down. Where there is overlap, you'll be able to further narrow down in the next step what it is you were born to do.

Question #1: What do I think about the most?
Granted, if you're a teenage boy, the answer might be sex, sports, or sex. And if you're a teenage girl, the answer might also be sex, sports, or sex. Heck—if you're of any age you could answer Question #1 with those three things. So, go ahead and get the selfish and recreational pursuits

out of your mind—unless you think those could indeed be your passion.

For example, you may think about fishing more than anything else. You go fishing each weekend and holiday, you watch fishing shows on TV, and all of your Facebook friends know you as "that guy who always posts status updates about fishing." Although this might seem like a recreational pursuit, it could also be a passion. So, don't dismiss something because it seems trivial or extracurricular. It could be the very thing you're meant to do.

The best way to tell whether what you think about the most is an actual passion or not will come in the next step: making a plan. I might think about movies a lot, but if I want to earn a living as an actor, part of my plan would be to study filmmaking, to perhaps even move to New York or Los Angeles, and to take as many acting classes as I can afford. If I'm honest with myself, that part of my plan might be completely unrealistic, so perhaps I'm not as passionate about movies. However, it doesn't mean that acting can't be a part of my passion in some way. During the planning stage, you'll start to think about your passion in more practical detail.

In terms of what you think about the most, think about which of those ideas is attainable and realistic. When it was time to dream, it was okay to dream big dreams. However, with a passion, it's time to focus on what's more doable and practical. If your potential passion involves some sort of physical, mental, or emotional requirement—although all three might be learnable with proper training—it's important to think of your passion as what you were born to do. Thus, some of us weren't born to play sports, work with people in extreme poverty, or perform heart transplants.

Right now, you might be thinking about a particular thing. Maybe you just watched a great movie or are drinking your favorite beverage. Thus, what you think about the most right now could be film- or coffee-related. Although it's important to make a note of that, neither may be much of a concern in two weeks' time.

Therefore, consider trying to answer this question over a period of time. Jot down each evening what you thought about the most over the course of the day. Do it each day for a week. Then, review it after seven days and see whether there were any consistent thoughts or themes. For greater accuracy and balance, do it for a month or over a period of time when you're doing different things, like working, vacationing, trying something new, or developing a routine. After all, countless people have vocalized a religious calling after just one unique and extraordinary spiritual experience.

Admittedly, the same set of things might truly occupy your thoughts. If you're a parent, a spouse, a supervisor, a teacher, or an artist, most of your days are occupied with similar thoughts. In fact, they have to be in order for you to excel at that role. Therefore, "most" might not be best measured in terms of quantity of time.

Instead, as you have free time, take note of where your

mind goes. If your downtime happens in the evening once the kids are tucked in, what is it that comes to mind? Or, if your commute to work is your best chance at alone time, are you pondering something in particular? Lying in bed at night, what do you think about? What's the first thing on your mind when you wake up? If you're willing to be fully in tune with your thoughts, you'll notice a pattern that develops, something you can't ignore, something that will start speaking to you.

Question #2: If I'm known for only one thing, what is it? You can answer this question in two ways:

- What you would currently be known for were you to not make it until tomorrow morning.
- What you'd like to be known for, assuming you get to live a long and normal life until a ripe old age.

The second scenario is how best to proceed with this question in mind, not just from an odds standpoint, but also because you'd be very busy changing or correcting the first option in order to get everything done by daybreak.

Your answers to this question might be a bit vague and might also hit on things not related to your career. That's okay. This question is designed to have you think in terms bigger than what you do for a living. Unless you're a captain of industry or a world-famous inventor, what you'll be known for doing as a career will probably go unknown in most circles.

Most of us want to be known as a loving husband, a great wife, a fantastic grandparent, a meaningful friend, or a great son or daughter. We might also want to be thought of as a reliable volunteer, a generous giver, or a visionary board member. Deep down, what is it you want to be known for?

By thinking about things outside of a simple career framework, you'll also be able to begin prioritizing. Not all of us are called to any particular career. Not all of us need to turn our passion into our profession. Some of us will actually do more good outside of our nine-to-five jobs as long as we're living out our passion in clear view of the legacy we hope to leave.

This question will also be best answered if you think about how you'd like to be known by different people. By thinking intentionally about these audiences, you'll also be honest about who means more to you. It's more important that your parents think of you as a fantastic son than your customers think of you as a smart marketer. And it's more important that your friends consider you as someone who's supportive than for strangers who read your Wikipedia entry to consider you as a strategic innovator.

Question #3: What do I value?

Most everyone has a moral compass. Most of society has an idea of right and wrong. But very few of us have a clearly defined set of values, those things that guide us to make decisions about what is right and wrong or what determines true north on our moral compass.

Perhaps it is a lack of knowing what we value that leads us down slippery slopes and morally ambiguous paths. Understanding what it is we treasure most and then making decisions in light of those priorities will enable us to stay on course when it comes to defining and then acting on our passion. Although value systems and even ethics can differ from one person to the next, making sure that we each have an understanding of our own system will help us discover what's important, what's worth spending time on, and where we are willing to make a stand—the three components of a clearly defined answer to this question.

What one person considers essential or urgent could be what another thinks is worthless or even comical. But if you're not sure what's important to you, you'll never have an idea of what you value, and you might never arrive at knowing what it is you were born to do. Think about what you place a priority on. What is it that you consider urgent, necessary, or deserving of your full attention? Is there a certain issue, news story, or idea that always captivates you and makes you stop what you're doing in order to fully engage? Is there something that will always motivate, inspire, or challenge you? If you were to list five things that you consider important, what would they be and why?

Another way to think about what you value is to take stock of what you spend time on. What in your life do you make sure to do right or do well regardless of the time it takes? What will you make sure to stay up late or wake up early in order to complete or accomplish?

Answering this question will also bring to light what it is you don't value. Then, you can begin to let those things go or fall to the wayside in order to better devote time and energy toward what it is you value and what you just might be meant to do. If we don't value or appreciate something and if we don't consider something important, then why spend time on it that we could otherwise devote to honing an existing talent, growing an essential resource, or further following our passion?

Along with considering something important and then spending time on it, we must think about where we're willing to take a stand. Although you could answer this question in political or religious terms, you could also answer it in terms of a social issue, a particular hobby, or an educational pursuit.

In other words, what do you correct others about when someone is misinformed? When are you willing to attach your name and identity to an opinion you have? When are you willing to stand alone, stick your neck out, or go out on a limb? What is it that motivates you to make a commitment and then invite others to make that same commitment?

By thinking deeply about this question and the three ideas that comprise it, you'll be better able to determine what strikes a chord somewhere deep within you and stirs that small voice inside to speak to you, to tell you what your life's work is.

Question #4: What must I do every day?

Although this question can seem a lot like the previous one, especially in terms of where you take a stand or how you spend your time, it's important to remember that action is often a key indicator of where we're passionate.

Taking a stand in the form of having and sharing an opinion (especially online) is one thing. Carving out time to focus on or think about something is another. But making sure to engage in an active, regular, and—best of all—daily discipline could help you more easily understand a passion.

Presumably, there are some things you do every day, like shower, eat, and breathe. You probably also go to work, pay bills, and are a responsible member of society most days, too. But for this question, think beyond what it is you have to do and more along the lines of what it is you can't *not* do.

What is it that you enjoy doing more than anything else? What is your favorite part of the day? What is it, after you do it, that you tell everyone about? Is there something that's a regular part of your day that you can't do without? Is there a certain routine that if interrupted throws you out of whack for the rest of the day?

Although there is a certain number of activities that you do every day that you love, be sure to think critically about this question. We all love spending time with friends and loved ones, and I hope you get to do this each day, whether it's in person or virtual. But it would be very hard to make a living at this or to even assume it as a passion. So, think carefully and thoughtfully about this question. What do you freely choose to do each day that is not required but that you feel must be a part of your day for it to be complete?

Question #5: What do I tell other people about myself?
Cocktail parties and mixers can be the worst places in the world to go if you're still trying to figure out your passion. Anywhere you go and are forced to meet new people, you'll be asked, "What do you do?"

This is, of course, a terrible question whether you're working your dream job or you're stuck in a career you hate. Most of us don't want to be defined in anyone's mind by what we do to earn a paycheck. Yet in a capitalist society, whether we want to acknowledge the economic realties of our social interactions or not, we're often left to define ourselves (and evaluate others) by the value we seem to be able to create for ourselves and for our communities as a whole.

So, if we're forced to answer, "I work at a job I hate," or, "I sit on the phone all day," or, "I do something that you think is stupid, meaningless, or insignificant," then we immediately hate the person asking, the event we're at, or ourselves. We could either decide never to go to parties or anywhere else we might meet someone we don't know, or we could change the question or the answer—or both.

When I meet new people, I like to ask either "What's your story?" or "What would you like me to know about you?" This way, if people want to tell me how they are able to pay their mortgage, so be it. But it also opens the door for connection on a deeper, more passionate level. It means that we can get past name tags or business cards and get down to what it is each of us cares about and spends time doing. Immediately, our sense of passion can come to the forefront.

You can answer this question by answering either of the ones that I ask at parties. What is your story? And what would you like a total stranger to know about you? Is it what you're passionate about or what you're called to do? Is it where you'd like to be or what you'd like to be remembered for? You'll also find that by answering these questions—whether at parties or on a sheet of paper—will allow for more meaningful conversations and connections, which is always time well spent.

Question #6: When do I feel fulfilled?

The reason I shy away from terms like "excitement" when talking about passion is because they can define something as very temporary. Even if our passions change over the course of our lifetimes, they take root in something much more permanent.

And that's why this question is about fulfillment instead of just when you feel happy or when you get excited. Fulfillment is a condition that can last a very long time. It's a deep-rooted feeling that brings a sense of accomplishment and completeness with it. It's something that can make us proud and leave us feeling like we did something that was worth doing to begin with.

Which behaviors or actions bring a sense of fulfillment for you? What do you do that, when you do it, makes you feel proud for having completed the task? What will you tell others later that you did today?

Knowing what brings fulfillment will help you prioritize how you spend your time (along with Question #3), which is important because when figuring out your passion and how exactly you'd like to do something with your one life, you'll need all the time you can get.

Step Three: Make a plan

Once you've taken your dreams and articulated them into a fistful of passions, it's time to set out a plan in order to turn these dreams into reality by using your passion, something that is uniquely yours. A plan enables you to take your big, wild-eyed dreams and morph them into something that can be seen, embraced, and used by others. Your plan is much more specific than a dream or a passion. Your plan lays out timelines, goals, tasks, and resources. It identifies all the pieces and parts you'll need as you seek to live out your dreams.

Planning can be scary because it makes things much more tangible. It makes your dreams feel more real, and this can make you nervous. What if you fail? What if your dream was off base? What if what you thought you were passionate about is no longer true?

Don't worry. You'll be able to modify your plan as needed. And the results of the plan might mean that you need to modify your dreams and passions. This is okay. After all, you need to know whether you need better or more accurate dreams. You, of all people, need to be informed if what you think is your passion is nothing more than a casual interest.

The great thing about a plan is that it will help you begin to see how possible and how quickly your dreams can be realized. You could go on dreaming forever. Although enjoyable and a great leisurely pursuit, if you only dream, they'll never come true. If all of your time is spent wishing—and not acting—nothing will ever come of it. Your dreams need your help and hard work in order to be made real.

In order to formulate a plan to see what you can produce, here are six questions to consider, each an integral part of your plan.

Question #1: What resources do I need?

You'll never be able to turn your dreams and passion into reality without getting together all the materials and resources to do so. You might need to learn a lot more. You might need to get your finances in order, save some money, or spend some money to truly live out your passion. You might also need a building, plane tickets, or an alligator farm (seriously—if you are very passionate about exotic reptiles). Making a list of what you need to do in order to get where you want to go will serve as a quick and easy checklist so you can begin to live out your dreams.

Question #2: How much time do I have?

One key factor in determining exactly how you'll begin to make your dreams come true is time. We all have a limited amount of it. Try as we might, we can never add hours to the day or even press pause. Time can't be slowed down; the clock keeps ticking regardless of all that we need to accomplish.

Therefore, accurately assessing how much time you have to spend on your dreams will determine what it is you'll do to make them happen. If you have time only on the weekends to work on developing your passion, then you'll take different steps than if you have more than forty hours a week to work on it. Likewise, thinking about how much time you have left will also provide valuable insight into the steps you need to take. Do you want to see your dreams realized before you have children? Before you get a graduate degree? Do you want to spend the next ten years living your dreams all out to see whether you have what it takes? Think about time on both a weekly and overall basis, and you'll know what steps to take next.

Question #3: Who do I need to know?

Dreams are never achieved alone. Just like there are

no true overnight successes (fame usually comes only after many years of hard work), there are no true solo acts.
People who have achieved great things always have a phe-
nomenal supporting cast behind them.

Therefore, it's important to realize that you'll need
help in living out your dreams in order to find what truly
matters to you. Who are the experts in your field? Who
has done what you're trying to do, and how can you learn
from them? What groups should you join? Who has written books on the topic you're dreaming about and can offer words of wisdom? Who has skills and talents that you
don't that will be valuable to you as you live out your passions and dreams?

Question #4: What's the first step?

It's important to identify the very first step you'll need
to take as you begin to put your passion into action. There
will be countless steps before you arrive at the end, but the
key is to identify what it is you need to do first. Sometimes,
it's the first step that's the hardest. As a runner, I know that
the most difficult step when jogging on a cold morning to
train for a half-marathon isn't the first step into the cold
air; it's the step out of bed. Leaving the comfy confines
of a warm bed is much harder than stepping into a brisk
breeze. But once I've gotten up, I find it easy to put my
shoes on, bundle up, and begin running.

I've also found that the first step might be the very
thing that keeps us going. When I ran my first marathon, I

found myself completely out of energy for the second half of the race. I kept plodding along, though, and eventually I made it to mile 23. When I did, I was reminded that the remaining distance (3.2 miles) was nearly the same as the first race I ever did many months earlier (which was a 5k, or 3.1 miles). Knowing that I had already accomplished it before gave me the fortitude to keep stumbling toward the marathon finish line.

You never know when the first step—whether it's writing a business plan, telling your story, or making new friends—will be the very thing you need to arrive at the threshold of achieving your dreams. Identify the first step in as much detail as possible so you can set everything into motion. I've found that living your passion is one big snowball of action-packed energy and surprises. But it will never be set in motion unless you take that first, all-important step.

Question #5: What's keeping me from acting?

Even when you've identified the first thing you'll need to do, fear, hesitation, and worry can keep you from acting. This is normal. If you've created a crisis moment for yourself and left a job or moved across the country, the prospect of failing or falling short can even make you nauseated. Embrace that fear; it means you're alive and you're ready to do something. Overcome this fear by realizing that doing nothing at all will produce even worse results than trying something.

Name your fears. Write them down. Figure out exactly what is stopping you from taking the first or any subsequent steps. Only when you name what it is that is preventing you from moving forward can you work to address it. We'll discuss obstacles in more detail when reviewing how to craft your personal strategic plan, but for now, simply try to understand what your biggest hesitations and hang-ups are.

A few reminders about passion

I speak and write about passion a lot, and when I do, I always remind people to keep these things in mind when trying to figure out what it is they're passionate about.

1. Your passion is a compass, not a map. It will point you in the right direction, but it won't offer turn-by-turn directions on how to get there.
2. Passions are like best friends; they'll change throughout your lifetime.
3. Passions are like pancakes; three or four are great, but any more and you'll be sick to your stomach.
4. Passions are like salt; we need just the right amount at the right time. Too much of a passion all at once and we'll get tired of it.
5. Passions can stay a hobby. Not everyone has to turn their passion into his or her profession. It works for some, but not for all.

Question #6: What's missing?

Look back over your answers to the previous five questions. What else do you need before taking action? What other ideas do you need to have? What questions need to be answered? Is there a key piece of your passion that's still undefined or too ambiguous? Find the link that's missing and then work to get it in place.

Step Four: Put the plan into action

It's time to get serious. You've spent time dreaming, narrowed those dreams into a few passions, and made your plans to see what it's like to live out these dreams. Now what?

Get busy.

Once your plan is complete, you need to put it into action. You can't sit idly by knowing what you need to do and not do it. Don't fall victim to "the bystander effect." This social psychological phenomenon showcases that when a crowd of people witness some kind of emergency or crisis, everyone thinks someone else will call for help. As a result, no one calls for help and everyone is a bystander. This confusing reality came to light in 1964 when Kitty Genovese was stabbed to death. It is claimed that 38 people heard her scream for help, but no one acted and called the police. You can't assume that anyone else will do what it takes to turn your dreams into reality. It's up to you to set things in motion and do the hard work required.

In this phase—the action phase—you're getting dirty, getting tired, and getting results. You owe it to yourself to see whether what you dream of can come to pass. You need

Passion or casual interest?

I see many people get distracted and set off course thinking that a casual interest is actually a passion. Based on a knee-jerk reaction, people start companies, make major life decisions, and change the way they live only to wind up regretting it. Don't make the same mistake. Being able to tell the difference between a passion and a casual interest could save you a lot of time, money, and regret.

Casual Interest	*Passion*
Came on strong and suddenly	Has been with you for years
Seems to go hand-in-hand with a cultural fad or movement	Is something you love regardless of what's popular at the moment
Does not align with a talent	Usually goes hand-in-hand with something you do well
Is not associated to be in tandem with you by other people	Is directly and easily associated with you by others

Is something purely fun and even a welcome distraction	Is fun, but cuts deeper to line up with an issue or topic that deeply inspires you
Doesn't always have to be a part of your day	Causes you to feel incomplete if too much time passes without working with or on it
Not worth taking a stand on	Always worth taking a stand on
Easily forgotten or overlooked	Nearly always at the forefront of your mind

to see what it's like to truly live out a passion, whether it's as a full-time job or in your spare time each evening and weekend. You have one life, and it's time to do something.

As you begin to work your plan, measure as much as you can. Just remember: if you can't measure it, it doesn't matter. During the action phase—when you finally begin to live out your hopes and dreams for a better life—evaluate as much as you can so you can make corrections as needed. Did one action step have the results you desired? Were you able to round up all the resources you needed as quickly as you hoped? What else do you need now? Constantly reflecting as you act out your plan will help you to plan better in the future.

To best measure your actions, here are six questions to ask yourself.

Question #1: What has been successful?

This question should be the easiest to answer. Success is usually easy to see, and it's something we all enjoy. Therefore, identifying what worked will come naturally. Make a list of all the great and happy things that have happened when you tried to live out your passions and achieve your dreams. Where did you receive praise from others? What felt great when you did it? How many goals did you achieve? You'll want to replicate what worked well so you can have continued success in the future.

Question #2: Where did I fall short?

Answering this question will require humility, but it's in your best interest to answer it completely and honestly. If something doesn't work, it doesn't need to be repeated. As Albert Einstein succinctly put it, "Insanity is doing the same thing over and over again and expecting different results." If something is not working, it doesn't need to be done again with different hopes; it needs to be done completely different so that it can have a chance to succeed next time. Without naming where you fell short, you'll never know what you need to abandon. The more quickly you stop doing what's not working, the quicker you'll have real success, which will make you happier and make your dreams come true much more quickly.

Question #3: What worked but could be modified to work better?

In addition to identifying what needs improving, you'll also want to note what needs modification. If something worked but can work better, make the necessary adjustments. If something could have been done bigger or better, say so. If something could have been done more cheaply, been less of a drain on your resources, or could have been made more efficient, say so and adapt. Living out your passion and chasing down your dreams is a journey you'll be on for the rest of your life; making changes along the way so you can keep traveling is wise.

Question #4: Who else needs to be involved?

Now that you've tried your hand at living the life you've always wanted, who else needs to come on board to lend a hand? In the previous step, as you planned you named people you needed to know and get involved. Since you have now had a go of it, who else needs to be a part of your team? Having seen your results, what input do you need? Who would you like to meet? Who has skills and talents that could be of use at this stage? The person you need is out there; you just need to know who you're looking for so you can find them.

Question #5: What have I learned?

Best of all, once you begin to truly take action on your dreams, you'll learn a lot. You'll learn even more about the industry you're working in, you'll learn skills and talents you didn't know you had, and best of all, you'll learn a lot about yourself. Ultimately, you're on a journey of personal development. Sure, you're trying to work in a job you love and make enough money to pay for the things you like. But you're also discovering what it is that matters to you. This is important because you can't live a simpler life until you know what you need more of. You can't get rid of things until you know you don't need them. Remember: a simple life isn't about decreasing volume; it's about balance and having as much of what you love as possible while getting rid of all the things you don't need. Learning about yourself will help you further plan ahead by knowing what you need to do more of and where you can use more help.

Question #6: Now what?
Press the repeat button.

Once you have answered these questions and then get to work, remember that the process is what matters here. Failure is okay. The point isn't to be perfect but to keep improving.

Another major reason to measure each step you take is so you can plan again. This entire process—from dreams to action—can be repeated over and over again throughout your life. If you have new dreams or think you have uncovered a new passion at some point that will help you achieve a dream, then plan and act again. Or, once you act on your current list of dreams and measure the results, re-plan and re-act if you still haven't made major progress. Don't give up if things didn't turn out like you hoped. Your dreams and passions are too important and unique to give up on. Don't scrap them; just come up with a better plan.

How long should this take?

This process seems extensive, but it's meant to be complete, not convenient. In our world of high-speed everything and instant gratification, if something can't happen instantly, we rarely have the patience to see it through. But your dreams and passions are important enough to be worked on thoroughly. Don't skimp on each step just because you need to finish everything before bedtime. Live deeply with all twenty-four of the previous questions. Think carefully about each answer and be proud of what you write down.

That said, you could easily come up with all four steps (dreams, passions, plan, action) in a few hours. To do it well and allow for more time for deeper reflection, you could spend a few weeks. Either way, the actual process of identification won't take too long. However, the process of putting it all into action could take substantially longer. In order for it to truly work well, I recommend taking the college approach and fitting it all in over four years.

That seems like a lifetime in our world that is always speeding up and encouraging speed over substance. Who cares how great something is when you can have it in an instant? Anything "cooked" in a microwave tastes medio-cre, but we don't seem to mind because it took only ninety seconds. Contrast the taste of a frozen burrito with how delicious Thanksgiving dinner is. Taking the time to do something right makes a difference.

I also suggest spending four years on this because our minds are good at using that amount of time to take a new, ambitious concept and break it down into more manage-able pieces. In fact, up until you graduate college, every-thing happens in four-year-long blocks. You stayed at home (or went to day care) for four (maybe five) years. Then, you had elementary school, middle school, and high school—all four years long. College was four years (for most of us). Spending four years working on bringing your dreams and passions into reality is a healthy and reason-able amount of time.

In the first year (starting right now), you're learning the ropes. You're figuring out the landscape of things and staying general. Let's say you're passionate about agricul-ture. There's no need to become an expert on the over fifty varieties of squash—this might never be valuable infor-mation when it comes to what you were truly meant to do. Agriculture, after all, can include anything from large-scale industrial meat production to local backyard tomato gardening, and plant mutations to organic composting. You could create a company that sells the most durable kind of gardening glove, or maybe you get your Ph.D. and teach at a large university.

Instead, spend a year learning about the various extensions of your passions. If you think you might want to start a company based on your passion, learn as much as you can about entrepreneurship. If you think you'll want to advocate for a cause related to your passion, learn how nonprofits or legislation works. Stay general and soak up as much information as you can. You can also use this time to meet as many new people as possible and learn how everything is laid out, like you did when you were a freshman. Who are the experts? Who can be trusted? Where is the "library" (the place you can go for more information)?

During your second year pursuing your passions, you'll want to start focusing a bit more and not spread yourself so thin. This is the time—like in college—to join clubs (except that in the adult world they're called interest or networking groups). What local organizations should you become a part of to learn more and meet the right people? Is there a chance for you to become a leader of any of these groups?

You'll also want to start thinking about a "major," or what you'll spend most of your time doing. If you're passionate about children, start thinking about whether that means you want to educate them or entertain them. Should you be a teacher or a clown? Either will allow you to work with children, but you'll need a very specific skill set for each one. Use the second year to even try your hand at various outlets for your passion. Observe a classroom and try on a red nose. Put yourself in the very shoes of those who already have careers like the one you think you want.

Year three is when you get really serious. You're going deeper now; the time for exploration has passed. If your passion is developing technological solutions for developing markets (like solar panels for African villages without electricity), then it's time to learn as much as you can about the location (which country in Africa) and the technology (what external factors will affect production) as you can. Specialize. Find someone who knows the most about the topic and get to know them. Start becoming an expert yourself.

This is also the time to test in more detail what you'd like to do. Visit the village you'd like to give the solar panels to. Work at the factory that makes them. Dream up a way to make the panels faster and cheaper. Test your assumptions—and the assumptions of others—and see what's worth building upon and worth destroying. Give yourself the room, power, and freedom to create. You're getting very serious about what you're doing; make sure you act like it.

At year four, you're nearly ready. You can articulate your passion in one clear sentence, and you know the next immediate extension of it. You've got a clear plan in place to start a business, get more formal education, apply to certain jobs, or continue to modify your current line of work. You know what you need to know (and then some) about your passion, and it's visible. It's coming to fruition.

Make sure you're doing something each day that touches on and builds on your passion. Tweak something when it doesn't work. Recognize failure and learn from it. Celebrate when something does work and share it with others. You've built a platform over the last four years that has garnered you a reputation as a resource and expert on what it is you're passionate about. Leverage that reputation to continue to bring your dreams into reality.

Looking back at it, four years can fly by. You can learn a lot in less than half a decade, if you're deliberate about it. And if it means you get to live your dream life—one that's full of passion and excitement—for the rest of your life, then four years is a drop in the bucket compared to the happiness that awaits you for the rest of your days.

Resist the urge to do something quickly, and instead, make sure you do it well.

5

creating your personal
strategic plan

5

creating your personal strategic plan

If you really want to be happy by finding work that matters and making sure you have enough of the right things in your life, you must develop a Personal Strategic Plan. Like the Dream to Action Plan, a Personal Strategic Plan is a key process that will help you continue to be reminded about what's important and get more of it in your life. Without it, you'll continue to fill your life with clutter and distractions.

Usually, strategic plans are developed over several months by companies and nonprofits. They often hire a team of consultants (at a hefty hourly rate) to help a board of directors and key leadership define what the organization should be doing. Most of the time, a well-done strategic plan helps set the agenda and trajectory of a company for the next three to five years.

A strategic plan is needed in business because it helps the leaders of the organization know when to say yes and what to say no to. Oftentimes, organizations can get sidetracked. A corporation will chase a dollar and a nonprofit will chase a cause without pausing to think whether doing so is in the best interest of the company. Just because you can do something doesn't mean you always should.

Therefore, a strategic plan allows the CEO to decline an offer to buy another company or start a new business unit if doing so isn't in line with the company's plan. It helps a nonprofit director steer clear of a new program that isn't on par with where the organization should be heading. Decisions become easier and more consistent. As a result, the organization becomes more effective, better run, and assured that it will continue to operate well for many years.

In the same way, you need a strategic plan for your life. Knowing who you want to be, what you want to do, and where you want to go will help you when you have tough decisions to make. Should you go back to school? Should you change jobs? Is it time to move? These decisions are weighty and should never be made in haste. A strategic plan for your life will help you make them in a way that isn't impulsive or reactionary.

I wish I had followed a strategic plan twice in life. Two times I've begun graduate school only to bow out a year later.

The first pass at graduate school was in California. My fiancé (now my wife) and best friend drove with me out to California, a multiday adventure that allowed us to see every inch of interstate between Tennessee and southern California. Thank God for great friends like Adam. Without him, I'd never have my boxes of books and heavy couch brought up two flights of stairs. I don't blame him for not moving me back to Tennessee six months later when I decided I didn't want an advanced degree.

I did well in my first semester of theology school, fresh out of college. I had a 3.8 GPA, but I wasn't sure what I wanted to do with my life when I was due to graduate in just eighteen months. Maybe I wanted to work in a church. I could see myself writing or working on a college campus. I thought working for a community-based organization like a nonprofit might be a good fit. Full of career possibilities, I headed to the career services office.

I laid out my options to the representative and asked whether she could help me get an internship in one of those areas. I felt that the only way to know what I'd love doing for a career was to give it a try. If I absolutely hated the day-in, day-out responsibilities of working in a church, then I could cross that off my list and move on to the next idea. Finding a career by process of elimination seemed much more practical than taking a personality test.

She listened to my ideas, and then stated, "That sounds like a good plan, and we do help students find internships. Unless you're a new student. You see, we only find place-ments for second-year students." I smiled politely, asked her if she could reconsider for an ambitious dreamer like myself, and even begged. She was unrelenting. Policy was policy. I thanked her for her time and walked directly down the hall to the dean's office to learn the process for withdrawing from school.

Why go into more debt and spend the next year and a half learning something that I might never use? How would I know what classes to take if I didn't know what I'd be using them for? In many ways, graduate school is like trade school; one should only go when they know what they'll be using the new degree for. If you want to be an attorney, you need to go to law school. A doctor? Go to med school. Barbers, journalists, professors—they all need highly specific extra schooling in order to land the job they want. If you don't know what you want to do, then why enroll? I signed up to get a master's degree because I had no strategic plan for my life. I was making big decisions based on what seemed right or what appealed to me at any given moment. Had I been thinking more deliberately, more clearly, and more strategically, I'd be able to know what I should have done, which was steer clear of graduate school. I could have started my first business years earlier and had a more relevant learning experience.

Instead, I left school, moved back to the town where I grew up, and worked at a hotel for two unhappy years before finally creating a crisis moment and saying good-bye to full-time work. It would still be years before I started

Cool People Care after finally discovering my passion. But I look back at my grad school "experiment" and business "education" at the expense of a major hotel chain wishing I could have done it differently. I'm grateful for each experience, but I might just trade it all in for a chance to have made more strategic and sensible decisions years earlier. Whether you're a college student, in the middle of your career, or staring retirement in the face, if you don't have a strategic plan, your life can get awfully cluttered and awfully stressful very quickly. Being deliberate about what you do and why will save you time, money, headaches, and even some regret.

And now, nearly five years later, a strategic plan for my life is finally in place. Now I know which opportunities to say yes to (believe it or not, graduate school is still a possibility), and which ones to decline. I'm able to take on projects that matter to me while politely saying no to those that don't align with the person I'm trying to be or the goals I'm trying to accomplish. Instead of saying yes on a whim, I'm deciding with focus and purpose. I'm happier—and life is much simpler—because of it.

In order to chart a career and life path that is best for you, you need to complete a Personal Strategic Plan. Having been a part of nonprofit strategic plans, I've modified the typical corporate strategic plan to apply more to individual life. There are still components that sound very businessy, but I explain them in a way that is relevant, worthwhile, meaningful, and easy to apply in your own life.

Take time to complete this plan. You can brainstorm and fill in many parts of it in an afternoon, but be sure to spend time reflecting on it. Just like the Dream to Action Plan, it's important to be honest with yourself in this process. Lying or not telling yourself the whole truth will only produce a personal strategic plan that is incomplete or irrelevant. Once you're done, be sure to review your plan regularly—I'd suggest every other month—and any time you face a major decision. Doing so will keep you on course to living the life you've always wanted.

Step One: Determine your values

The first step in creating a personal strategic plan is to list your values. What is it that you value? What is important to you? What serves as your moral compass, your true north, when it comes to ethics and values?

These don't have to be complete sentences. Simply find a piece of blank paper and start writing. Single words or short phrases are great. Set a timer and list everything you value for five uninterrupted minutes. Look back at how you answered the values question when trying to define your passion while developing your Dream to Action Plan. Then, take a break. Go for a walk, go to work, take a nap. Come back later in the day and do the same thing for five minutes on a new sheet of paper. Then, compare each sheet. If something made each list, circle it and write it again on another sheet of paper.

What made both lists? How many do you have? The number isn't important—you can have as many as 100 or as few as five. If you have a lot, you'll whittle them down in the next step. If you have a few, the next step will be even easier.

Now that you have your list of values, it's time to organize them and identify the common themes. I've found that after the first attempt at writing down your values, most people will have listed fifteen to twenty-five. Again, if you have a lot more or a lot less, don't worry. As long as you were honest and complete in listing your values, however many you have is the right number for you.

Your next goal is to take those values and whittle them down to five.

Find a set of sticky notes and write each value from your list on its own sheet. Once you've done this, find a blank wall or table and stick the notes to it. Now that you can see them all in front of you, begin to group them by those that are similar. For example, if you have "family" on one note and "friends" on another, you can put those notes near one another because both relate to people. If you have "volunteering" and "making a difference," those can be grouped together as well.

Take as long as you need to group things together. Some values may stand on their own; some groups may have ten of your values in them. You can create as many groups as you want, but ideally, you want between four and six distinct groupings.

What is a value?

A value is something important to you that's easily seen or consistently lived out. Think about what you spend time doing or thinking about during any given day. Some examples of values are:

Family
Friends
Faith
Caring for others
Being nice
Truthfulness
Passion
Work that matters
Making a difference
Sports

They don't all have to be highly moralistic or even whimsical. Don't be embarrassed if you wrote down that you value vampire movies or playing eighteen holes at expensive golf courses. If you like it, love it, or think about it often, write it down. It's important that you really get in touch with what matters to you. The values you settle on at the end of this step will help shape the rest of the process, so it's very important that you capture these as accurately as possible.

Once you have created your groups, look at each one separately. Read each note to yourself in that group. Close your eyes. Try to remember what you just read. Open your eyes and read them to yourself again. Now, come up with a name or a title for that group. For example, the group that contained your values of friends and family could be called "people" or "people close to me" or even "people that matter the most." If you had a group that included "fitness," "time with friends," "hobbies," and "learning new things," you may title that group "Leisure," or even "Things that make me happy." Again, the grouping of the passions and the titles of the groupings are up to you.

Once you've titled each group on a separate sticky note, put the note at the top of its corresponding group on the wall or on the table. Read back over the group title and each value in the group. Does the title accurately capture the grouping? If not, rename the group or regroup the values. Make sure you're happy and can remember each group heading.

Then, walk away. Wait four days.

After this period, pull out all the notes again. Reread them. Do the group headings still apply? Do you still feel as though everything is grouped correctly? If not, redo this process until you're happy with it. Do it as many times as you need until you feel it is 100 percent accurate upon revisiting it a few days later.

Once the labeling is accurate, gather your sticky notes with the group headings on them. Lay those out before you on a wall or table. Read each one out loud with the phrase "I value" in front of it.

"I value the people closest to me."

"I value spending time on things that matter."

"I value living life to the fullest."

"I value caring for others."

How do they sound? Do they reflect who you are? If so, congratulations! You've just articulated what it is you value. You can now easily say in just a few phrases what matters the most to you.

Once you have accurately articulated your values, you need to capture how you live out those values. This is where you can refer back to the two sheets of paper you used to list all of your values at the very beginning of this step.

Begin with a blank document on your computer or sheet of paper. List your values (4-6) and leave room under each to list ways you want to live out these values. In other words, how could someone see that you value what you do? If you value the people closest to you, what does that look like? Perhaps it means spending time with them frequently, going to dinner with a good friend once a week, or telling your family members each day that you love them. You can list as many ways as you like; the only requirement is that they must be evident. Don't merely list that you value people because you love them. List that you value them and you'll tell them you love them or show them you care. Pretend you're trying to prove that you value these things to someone who doesn't know anything about you.

Once you've done this for each value, print your document and place it or your handwritten sheet somewhere you can view it often. Being reminded of what you value never hurts, and seeing how you need to be demonstrating what you value will also be a handy reminder to live your life in such a way that you prioritize what you value. After all, they're called "values" because they mean something to you. They are valuable in some way. And valuable things tend to be treated very differently than something that has no or little value to you.

Living a simpler life is much easier done when you spend time on the right things—the things you value. This list of your values and how you'll live them will ensure you easily and quickly focus on what matters and let go of what doesn't. Now that you have defined your values, you can easily recall what is worth doing when approached with a new opportunity. Now, you can move on to the next part of developing your Personal Strategic Plan.

This next part of developing your Personal Strategic Plan is best done in tandem with someone else, either a mentor or someone from your brain trust (see chapter six for more information about each of these). Involving either will make this step stronger and more relevant, but it will take a lot of humility on your part. In the end, it will be worth it, and your Personal Strategic Plan will be better as a result.

This step in the process is called a SWOT analysis. SWOT stands for Strengths, Weaknesses, Opportunities, and Threats. Organizations identify each of these so that they can begin planning tactically what to do over the next three to five years. Similarly, it's important to identify these four areas in your life in order to:

- Capitalize on your strengths
- Minimize your weaknesses
- Take advantage of opportunities
- Neutralize threats

None of the above is possible without first identifying these four areas completely.

Step Two: Identify your strengths

In order to effectively and completely name all of your strengths, it's important to do so with a partner. Getting input on what you do well is gratifying. It will certainly boost your morale and confidence to hear about all of the things you do well. Just like listing your values, spend five uninterrupted minutes listing as many strengths as you can think of. Here are some questions to consider when doing so:

- What do you do well?
- What do you do better than anyone else?
- What have you been acknowledged for doing well?
- When do others pay you compliments?

List as many strengths as you can think of in five minutes and have someone who knows you well do the same. When you and your friend have completed your list, write all of them down on a single sheet of paper (you can use more than one sheet if needed). Then, go though each strength one by one.

If there are some strengths that each of you listed, there is no need to repeat them. Simply place a check mark by those that each of you listed. As you go over each strength, be sure to discuss it. What is it about that strength that you like? How do you know that what you listed is in fact a strength?

After you have discussed each strength from the list, each of you get to pick ones that you feel are better than others. In order to do that, ask yourself this question: "Which of these strengths, if focused on further, will take me where I want to go?" Because it is impossible to focus on forty strengths, you need to pick ten that you will further develop in the next few years. That doesn't mean the other thirty strengths that made the list disappear or are neglected; this simply means that you're choosing ten that are worth diving into deeper in order to progress your life and career.

To select the strengths worth pursuing from your entire list, you and a friend will each get seven votes. Go through the list again and make note on a separate sheet of paper seven strengths you feel are most worth further developing in order to take you where you want to go and be the person you'd like to be. Once you and your partner have voted, share your selections, making a note of them on the master sheet of paper. Circle the ones that received the most votes.

Now, of the strengths that received any votes, it's time to rank them in order. First choose the strengths that each of you chose. Decide among those by voting only among them. For example, if you came up with three strengths that overlapped, look at those three and rank them on your sheet of paper. Have your partner do the same. If your rankings match, then you now know the order; if they don't, have a discussion as to why each of you ranked them the way you did until you arrive at a consensus. If no agreement can be reached, then the final vote rests with you. This is your Personal Strategic Plan, after all.

Then repeat this process with the rest of the strengths that garnered votes until you've ranked all of your strengths—up to ten—that you are willing to develop and capitalize on. Make a list of these on another sheet of paper and place it with your four values to review frequently.

Here's an example of what your strength sheet should look like:

- Coming up with practical solutions to problems
- Making people feel welcome
- Generating excitement about something new
- Having effective writing and communication skills
- Remembering minute details
- Recognizing when other people need help
- Using humor to help diffuse a tense situation
- Synthesizing a lot of information quickly

- Learning about new things
- Playing the cello

Many times we're led to believe that we need to turn weaknesses into strengths and that strengths are fine as they are without further development. This is misguided thinking. Many weaknesses need to be abandoned and never focused on again. If you're not good at accounting, you don't need to work with numbers until you are. There are plenty of people who are great at accounting and will help you when you need it. Your time is better spent taking something you're already good at and becoming great at it, instead of taking something you're terrible at and becoming mediocre at best. The world never prizes mediocrity, but it does love people who can do things better than anyone else. It's better to do hundreds of things awfully and a few things great than thousands of things just so-so. Your ten strengths are about to become your focus areas for the next few years.

Step Three: Identify your weaknesses

Your weaknesses, on the other hand, need to be minimized. You first need to accurately recognize what they are. After all, it will be very difficult to stop doing something if you don't even know you're doing it. In order to best identify your weaknesses, you'll need to again find someone who knows you well. Ideally, this will be the same person who helped you identify your strengths, and these two exercises can be performed consecutively. You can easily take care of them over the course of a few hours one afternoon or during a very long lunch.

The process for naming your weaknesses is identical to identifying your strengths. Both you and a partner make your own lists; then make a master sheet with both of your ideas on it. Vote on this overall list by choosing seven items that answer this question: "Which of these, if not addressed, will quickly prohibit me from going where I want to be?" In other words, which of these could lead to your downfall? Which weaknesses, if you just ignore them, will prevent you from using a strength to become the kind of person you want to be? You can easily see why weaknesses need to be identified and addressed: they could single-handedly stop you from being who you want to be.

Once you have come up with your ten weaknesses, list those on a single sheet and place it with your values sheet and strengths sheet. You will need to keep these weaknesses top of mind in order to recognize when they pose a danger of preventing you from making progress in life. Here's an example of what your ten weaknesses could be:

- Getting distracted from the big picture by worrying about small details
- Not forgiving easily
- Being bad with money
- Having trouble respecting authority

- Not working well on a team
- Not respecting deadlines
- Being unable to articulate key ideas
- Finding it hard to get to the root cause of a problem
- Making too many impulsive decisions
- Deflecting acknowledgments and compliments to others too often

As you can imagine, listing your weaknesses is a humbling experience. It can be even downright depressing. This is why it's important to do this with someone who knows you well and whom you respect. They'll be honest with you, and they'll also laugh with you at your own shortcomings. They'll even recognize when you need a pep talk during the process, which can be very helpful.

The other thing to remember is that you should keep a list of these along with your values and strengths. Although burning your list or putting it into an empty bottle to toss out to sea can be symbolic, it also doesn't help you. These are things you actually want to keep in mind. Ignoring them will directly prohibit you from going where you want to go.

But it doesn't mean you work on these to improve them, like you do with strengths. It simply means you recognize when a situation might cause one of these weaknesses to surface. When that moment arises, you minimize the weaknesses in it by calling upon someone or something to lend a hand. If you face a chance to land your dream job, but part of the job requires you to concisely articulate key ideas, instead of you bungling those chances, find someone else on your team who does that well. Remember, you don't have to be great at everything. In fact, being awesome at a whole host of things can make life very complicated, and one of the goals of a Personal Strategic Plan is to make life simpler by correctly capturing what matters to you.

Step Four: Identify opportunities

Now it's time to identify the opportunities in your life. Like the phase in which you listed and refined your values, this portion can be done alone; there is no need to involve someone else unless you'd really like his or her input. The goal of this phase is to make you aware of the opportunities in front of you so you can use your strengths to make the most of them. Making the most of any given opportunity is what can catapult you to greatness. Opportunity knocks for all of us; those who end up doing what they love and simplifying their lives are those who take advantage of the right opportunities.

In order to best identify your opportunities, take a look at the sheet with your ten strengths on it. You'll need to refer to that sheet repeatedly during this phase. The key is to see which strengths can immediately present an opportunity. Certainly you will have other opportunities present themselves. Many events and occasions will fall into your lap, and you'll need to decide if they're worth your time and attention to pursue. In articulating your opportunities, however, we're not talking about the opportunities you can't control, those that appear as if from nowhere. Rather, we're focusing on the opportunities you can create for yourself.

So, take a look at your strengths sheet. Look at each strength carefully, and read every one out loud to yourself. As you do, think about your current circumstances. Think about the people and places you surround yourself with every day. Think about where you work, your family, your circle of friends, your neighborhood, and your place of worship. Think about your gym, any clubs or groups you belong to, where you volunteer, and places you like to go. Each place and each group of people is rife with opportunity, if you're willing to find it.

The trick here is to merge a strength with a place or a group in order to present yourself with an opportunity. Where can you use a strength that you currently are not using? Who needs what you can offer? Which group can you help with what you do best? Each of these is an opportunity for you to discover something you love doing in order to further develop a strength and even create a possibility for a door to be opened.

For example, if you're great at public speaking, where can you do that more often? Does your church need someone to preach when your pastor is away? Does a nonprofit group need someone to motivate its employees? Can you advocate for something in your neighborhood? All of these are opportunities you need to take advantage of by using one of your strengths. They will not present themselves; you need to go and create them.

Try your best to come up with two opportunities for each strength, and be as specific as possible. Don't just list that someone could use your graphic design skills. Instead, list who can use them (write down the name of the individual or the organization) and which skills you'll be using (laying out a newsletter, designing a poster, styling a Web site) to accomplish something specific. The more specific you are, the better off you'll be in rightly recognizing an opportunity that is directly in front of you. Opportunities are more easily taken advantage of when you can be very clear about what they are.

Once you have listed two (or more, but not more than four) opportunities for each strength, reconcile that list by writing it in its entirety on another sheet of paper to place with your values, your strengths, and your weaknesses. This plan, as you can see, is becoming quite a compilation. You'll need everything together so you can refer to it quickly.

As you can imagine, this is the only part we've done so far that will need to be redone regularly. Once you have taken advantage of all twenty (or so) opportunities, you'll need to brainstorm twenty more. Ideally, it will take you no more than six months to try out every opportunity that you list. Once you do, you'll have had a host of new experiences that will lead to even more opportunities. Instead of waiting around for opportunity to knock, you will have found where it lived and knocked on its door.

Step Five: Identify threats

Any business, organization, group, or idea has threats that can hamper its success. Threats are different from weaknesses, however, because they exist from the outside. You can think of internal weaknesses that can inhibit your progress; threats do the same externally. Weaknesses can be minimized; threats have to be dealt with and neutralized.

For example, one threat to Facebook's business model would be other networking companies starting up and trying to take its users. To deal with this threat, Facebook must continually improve in order to retain its user base. Luckily, one of Facebook's strengths is innovation, so it is always working to improve its site features in order to provide the best user experience to its members.

Or, a threat to a local community college might be that many high school students are deciding not to attend college because they see it as too expensive. To neutralize this threat, the college can start a public awareness campaign to show students how affordable community college can be and why getting a degree will increase one's future lifetime earnings drastically. It could then set out to have people give talks at local high schools or offer a place online where teenagers can ask questions about finances and college.

A threat for you, then, could be that your company is downsizing and you might get laid off. In order to deal with this threat, you'll need to showcase your strengths more in the workplace so you can be seen as indispensable. Or you might choose to start applying with other firms or networking with more people in your industry so you can step into a pivotal role at a new office should you be let go.

With that in mind, make a list of threats you see coming toward you. Again, think externally; consider things that are beyond your control. Is your industry dying? Are more people competing for fewer jobs? Is there a preconceived notion in the community about what you do that needs to be corrected? Think about things that pose a threat to using your strengths to take you farther and faster to where you'd like to go. You don't have to limit this to your job. If one of your strengths is painting, and you do this as a hobby, a potential threat could be that the price of paint and canvas is rapidly increasing, and you'll be forced to paint less. You can neutralize this threat by shopping for supplies in bulk, cutting something out of your life to save money, or using less expensive materials in your craft.

Once you list your threats, you'll need to list a brief plan to attack each one. These are things that should be top priorities. Remember, if these threats are not addressed, they'll drastically prohibit—if not entirely stop—any progress you'd like to make to live the life you always wanted. These threats must be named and neutralized.

So, just as you're making progress to take advantage of

the opportunities you listed, you'll want to use your time to also deal with your list of threats. Again, it's important to tackle as many as possible as quickly as possible. Take no more than six months to take care of all the ones on your list. After that time, make another list and continue to minimize the threats in your life. Doing so will keep you on track and ensure an unforeseen circumstance doesn't stand in the way of you and your dreams.

After completing this stage, you'll be done with your SWOT analysis, which will consist of four sheets of paper:

- A list of ten strengths
- A list of ten weaknesses
- A list of twenty opportunities you can create in the next six months
- A list of twenty threats to neutralize in the next six months

Normally, a company or nonprofit would now move on and spend as much time listing tactics (what it will literally do to capitalize on its strengths, minimize its weaknesses, take advantage of opportunities, and neutralize threats), metrics (how it will measure its tactics to know when it has been successful), and measurement (looking at the data to see how it did in addressing each part of its SWOT analysis). But companies don't have a Dream to Action Plan like you do. Luckily, your Dream to Action Plan covers most of this, particularly in the planning and action stage. In order to begin living out your passion, you'll need to set a plan and take action. As discussed, you'll regularly review the actions you took to see what worked and what will need to be done differently in the future.

Best of all, the Personal Strategic Plan highlights for you (without being bogged down in the minutiae of metrics and data) what truly matters. You now know what's important and how to use your best qualities to create opportunities to further become the type of person you dream of being. With your Dream to Action Plan (what you're doing) and your Personal Strategic Plan (what truly matters) in hand, you're now ready to get down to the details of simplifying your life, first by getting rid of clutter and then by getting rid of stress.

Here's an abbreviated version of what your opportunity sheet should look like:

Strength: *Able to connect people so they achieve a common goal*

Opportunity one: Introduce two songwriters from my breakfast networking group to see whether they can work on a song together

Opportunity two: Send an e-mail to Ben letting him know that he should have coffee with Selena; she has a business that can help him save money on invoicing

Strength: *Can see new business opportunities well*

Opportunity one: Investigate the feasibility of a new restaurant downtown

Opportunity two: Check in with Brad G. to see whether he is still considering opening a tutoring center near the college

Opportunity three: Schedule lunch with Lynnette D. to brainstorm new ideas for each of our companies

6

de-cluttering in order to focus on what matters

6

de-cluttering in order to focus on what matters

Your life is too full of stuff. You can easily go through your house and toss out fifty things, I bet (see my previous book on how to do exactly this). But our lives are full of clutter, too. Opportunities, projects, meetings, committees—there are too many things that we have no business being a part of because they don't play to our strengths or present opportunities for us to live out the values and dreams we've created for ourselves.

It's happened to me. At work or in the community, I'm often asked to volunteer in some way or attend a certain meeting. It feels great to be liked, so I have immediately said "Yes!" several times without even examining the opportunity to see whether it's the right fit—whether it's worth my time and energy to do well at something that will help me capitalize on a strength or create an opportunity in some way. It's easy to say yes, and to say it quickly. But the first step in de-cluttering your life in order to focus on what matters is to say no. A lot.

How do you say no?

Turning down stuff, opportunities, relationships, and any offer of "extra" certainly keeps your life less burdened and much lighter. But it can also make it boring and lonely. After having charted your dreams and passions and developed your Personal Strategic Plan, you now have a very detailed and useful blueprint to know what should be in your life. You can clearly articulate where you're headed, the kind of person you want to be, and the type of life you want to live, free from distractions, clutter, and almost anything unnecessary.

Therefore, you now know that you can say no. In fact, you now know that you *must* say no. If you don't decline something that interferes with your dream life, you're sacrificing a lot just so you don't have to hurt someone's feelings. You can still be seen as a nice person, even when saying no. But how exactly can you start turning people down, especially if you've spent your entire life quickly saying yes, even if it wasn't in your best interest and made your life anything but simple?

Follow these easy steps, and saying no will be easier than ever.

- *Be polite.* Saying no is probably bad news to the person asking. Make sure you tell them nicely. If you're in person, be sure to smile.
- *Tell them that you're honored to have been asked.* Confirm that person's hunch (and make them feel smart) that you were the right person to ask. You don't have to gush; saying, "Thank you so much for considering me," "I feel honored that you asked," or "It's so kind of you to want to work with me," will do.
- *Use the word no.* Using phrases like "This isn't the right time," "That opportunity seems like a lot," or "I'm not sure I'm able to do this right now," aren't technically nos. After you thank the person, be sure to say the word no. Get it in there. Be direct. That way, they know you officially declined the offer, and they can move on. Using the word no benefits both you and them.
- *Give a reason.* You don't have to spill your guts, but being honest about why you're saying no is a nice courtesy to pay and ensures that they will come back to you with another opportunity that could be more fitting and in line with your Personal Strategic Plan. The more specific you are, the more appreciative the other party will be. Phrases like,

"It's not the right season for me," or "I'm unable to participate at this time," are too vague; the person asking knows you're chickening out. Instead, give a real reason. Say that the opportunity doesn't line up with your Personal Strategic Plan. Let them know that it's not capitalizing on one of your strengths. Tell them that the offer as stated isn't one that you can spend time on since you're only focusing on opportunities to improve your life. Being honest and up front like this will actually start bringing the right opportunities along. Once people know which offers to bring you, you'll get more of the right ones, and you'll say no less. People will stop wasting time with the wrong offers and dream up something for you that fits.

- *Offer another option.* If you know someone who would be a fit for the committee, or who would love to volunteer, or who likes meetings—and you know they don't mind you sharing their name—offer an alternative. Letting the person know that you're not the right fit while telling them who is will ensure that no bridges are burned and that you're also a good source of information and connections. You'll stay in everyone's good graces even when saying no.

- *See how else you can help.* Ending the rejection with "How else can I help?" shows that you're still interested, you're still a friend, and you're still eager to lend a hand. Now that you've explained what opportunities you are looking for, you might get a more relevant one on the spot. It could also open more doors to other relationships. Even if you're not a good fit for this person, you might be the perfect fit for someone else she knows about.

Ultimately, it takes practice. The more you say no, the better you'll get. But, as I've mentioned, the better you get, the less you'll need to say it because the wrong opportunities will begin to steer themselves clear of you.

Here's an example of a "no" that takes into account all of the above principles. It's yours to use as you see fit. Copy and paste at your leisure—you're welcome!

Hi Stephen:

Thanks for your e-mail yesterday about serving on the fund-raising committee at Lindley's school. It means a lot that you think I have the skills to contribute. Unfortunately, I need to say no to this opportunity right now. This year, I'm only able to take on new projects that are directly in line with my strongest talents, which are marketing, public speaking, and strategic thinking. If you think there's a chance to use me in these areas, I'm all ears!

I would also like to mention Ann P. to you—have you met her yet? She used to fund-raise for a nonprofit before her family moved to town. She could be a great fit and was asking about ways to help the school just last week. Would you like her phone number or e-mail?

Thanks again,

Sam

When do you say yes?

Saying yes, of course, is usually much easier and much more fun. I don't offer a copy-and-e-mail template for saying yes; feel free to experiment all you want and use as many exclamation points as you like. The key with saying yes isn't how to say it, but rather when to say it. The answer is easier said than done: only say yes when it is in line with your Personal Strategic Plan that will help you live your passion and values. Anything else can be declined.

The same can be said to "stuff." When buying something or bringing something home, consider whether it will help you get where you need to go. A new cell phone or laptop sure would be nice, but if they aren't tools that will help you live a better, simpler life, then they're just toys that can easily distract you from more important goals.

In looking at stuff (material possessions, belongings, sentimental keepsakes), I offer two suggestions that will help you know when to say yes. Owning the right things will keep your life and house free of clutter, which will make you much happier and freer of stress. You'll also be able to take advantage of the right opportunities much more quickly.

1. *Utility vs. idolatry*

Before I make a major purchase—or these days, any purchase, for that matter—I ask myself, "Is this a tool to be used, or something I'll only end up idolizing?" There's a fine line between utility and idolatry, especially in our world of twenty-four-hours-a-day advertising, where any and every product offers some kind of health or happiness benefit. Watching just two minutes of any infomercial will leave you wondering how we ever got along without blankets with sleeves or magical blenders. Life must have been so hard and meaningless for our grandparents!

Don't rely on the promises of advertisers to determine whether something is useful for you. Companies will always tell you that their product is the one you're looking for and meets any need you have. They're not necessarily lying—a hammer that doubles as a screwdriver and has an extra guitar feature does sound useful. But if you rarely hammer or strum the guitar, it's just a waste of your time and money, even if it is cheap.

In order to determine whether something is useful for you, you'll need to first complete your Personal Strategic Plan. Then, when analyzing whether to spend money on something, examine your plan to see where this could help you—how it could make something easier, faster, or more efficient. If a set of nice cookware will be an asset when it comes to getting your dream of a catering business up and running, it seems like a good fit. But if you'll just marvel at the pots and pans and stack them next to three other sets, it seems they'll become more of a distraction or something to be ogled at than something that will be put to good use.

Of course, you don't have to do this with every purchase—that could get quite tedious. I highly doubt going to the movies or getting some ice cream is in line with too many strategic plans, but everyone needs some entertainment. Like all rules, even this one isn't meant to be taken literally all the time. Just ask yourself: will I use this, or worship it? Worshiping something leads to distraction; distraction leads to clutter; and clutter will take your focus away from living a simpler, better, more meaningful life.

2. *Twenty-four-hour waiting period*

The second thing I do, especially in making a major purchase (which I define as more than $100), is sleep on it. If I see a great looking couch, a new digital gadget, or a fun vacation idea, before I pull out the credit card, I impose a mandatory twenty-four-hour waiting period. It takes three days to buy a gun, but anyone can drive off the lot with a carload of debt.

Waiting makes me sure that I really want it (if I've already determined I actually need it). If it turns out that I'm not as excited about it, or the couch isn't exactly the color I thought it was, then I've saved myself some time and money. I can also make sure I don't fall victim to impulse buys. These knee-jerk shopping reactions are the reasons our homes are overflowing with stuff we don't need in the first place.

In fact, if I'm in need of a major purchase (a washing machine, a new TV, or a suit), I'll go shopping without any money. That way, I'll make sure not to fall prey to any savvy sales tactics, even if "the price could go up tomorrow," as those tricky salespersons like to say. That way, I'll be sure to come home empty-handed to first think on what it was I wanted to buy. This process has saved me countless times from buying something I don't need. Most of the time, what I think I want is only a distraction—good thing I didn't pay hard-earned money for it. Life is simpler when you buy only what you need and what you really want.

Why is free so expensive?

Marketers are geniuses. Seriously—it's like they know what I want before I do. And now, with the ability to target deals and advertisements more directly to me based on personal information or where I live, the temptation to buy things—especially discounted things—has never been greater. By now, nearly everyone has heard of Groupon or any one of its many competitors. Offering "collective buying," these daily deal Web sites send an e-mail to you each morning with a discount on a local service. With a few clicks you can be well on your way to learning how to sword fight, getting a great deal on teeth whitening, or enrolling in a fitness boot camp.

Sure, the prices have never been lower, but the cost has never been higher. Just because you can buy something for 75 percent off doesn't mean that you should. Learning how to hula-hoop might seem like a bargain for such a low price, but if you wouldn't have paid full price for it, how much were you interested in it to begin with? Sometimes, buying something—even if it's free or very cheap—can only lead to distraction and clutter.

The key is to beat the marketers at their own game. In order to avoid the temptation to buy more stuff you don't need, simply unsubscribe from these e-mails. It's your choice to have the daily deals delivered to your inbox; likewise, you can choose to not receive them. With one click of the mouse, you've simplified your life and gotten rid of a very enticing distraction.

The other way to simplify your life when it comes to these salacious offerings is to begin to say no to free things. In our world where everyone is trying to make a buck, getting something for free always seems like a bargain. But not everything that comes for free is worth it. In order to simplify your life, start saying no to free things.

I witnessed a great example of this while listening to Yvon Chouinard, founder of the Patagonia clothing company and my personal hero, give a keynote address. In talking about how businesses can help save the world, Chouinard discussed how our economy is built upon consumption, on the buying of more and more stuff by more and more people. Ultimately, he concluded, this is unsustainable and should not be encouraged.

At the end of his speech, the conference organizer came on stage to publicly thank him for his time and offered him a token of appreciation: a small gift bag with a travel coffee mug, some chocolate, and a few other small items like pens, magnets, and keychains. Instead of saying thank you and taking the bag of goodies, Chouinard actually said, "No, thank you. I already have everything I need." I—and the thousands of people in attendance—was impressed. The personal consistency of this man was to be admired. He rallied against consumption and then backed it up with his actions. Certainly this was a man whose life was simple and manageable because he declined what he didn't need, especially when it was free!

And how right he was. How many of us right now actually need another coffee mug or keychain? There's a key lesson for us here. If we don't need it, we need to decline it, even when it's free or cheap. Even if we don't pay anything for it, owning it could be a distraction. This is how drug dealers and food samplers at big-box retailers work: offer a free taste (who would decline free?) and gain a new customer for a very long time. In order to simplify your life, ask yourself these three questions before you say yes to something that seems like a great deal:

1. Would I have actually paid for this?

If you wouldn't have paid or paid full price for the item or service, you don't need it. Deep down, you might not even want it. Look past the price tag and figure out if this is something your life truly needs. Make sure you know which side of the utility-idolatry line this item is on.

2. What is the total cost of owning this item?

Free kittens and puppies seem like a bargain, but when you pick one up from a neighbor or family member, you're also picking up thousands of dollars in vet and food costs. The same goes for cars, computers, and cell phones. Nothing is ever truly free when you take into account the cost needed to maintain or manage what you're being given. Do the math and put the item back on the shelf.

3. Will I use this a year from now?

Many times, when we are given something for free, we appreciate it less. Because we didn't pay anything for it, it's less valuable to us. We made no sacrifice to acquire it, so it's reasonable that we're not very attached to it. I'm reminded of the story a former summer camp director told me. He was picking his eight-year-old son up from school one afternoon and saw him playing with friends and sliding in the school yard, getting grass stains all over his brand-new khaki pants. When his son was in the car, he asked him, "Why did you get grass stains all over your brand-new pants?" His son matter-of-factly replied, "I didn't pay for them." To his son, what he did with the pants didn't matter because it cost him nothing to get them.

Likewise, free promotional items such as towels, T-shirts, and other trinkets mean very little to you. You won't be using these things in a year (or even next week), so accepting them only creates clutter you will inevitably need to spend time getting rid of. When you say yes to the 5k T-shirt or the credit-card-offer beach towel, you're really just giving yourself a future chore. Say no to these free items and say yes to a simpler life.

Clear it all out

Now that you know how to make sure new items don't overwhelm you, how can you whittle down the current clutter taking up space in your home, office, car, and everywhere else you're at on a regular basis? Here are ten easy reminders that will help you eliminate what you don't need so you can live a simpler life. (If you'd like specific examples of what your life doesn't need, pick up my first book, *50 Things Your Life Doesn't Need.*)

1. *If it hasn't been used in the past year, you don't need it.*

This is an easy place to start, especially if you're standing in your closet right now. Or your kitchen. Or the den. Actually, no matter where you are, you're in a great place to start.

Take a look at your closet. How many items do you own that you haven't worn in a year or more? Chances are, these same items no longer fit. And while you have high hopes that they one day will, you'll be a lot happier thumbing through clothes that make you look great each morning before work rather than passing over item after item that makes you feel bad. Take stock of what's hanging up and what's in drawers and get rid of anything you haven't worn in a year.

Another prime place to look is your kitchen. Open all the cabinets and grab appliances and dishes that haven't seen the light of day since before Obama was elected. You may feel a tinge of guilt depending upon how much you spent to acquire these items, but despite your best intentions, your kitchen is full of unused items that can be donated and put to good use by someone else.

Check your living room. What DVDs have you not watched recently? Go to your garage and pull out old tools and gadgets that you haven't needed in who knows how long. Look in your bathroom for unused towels and linens. Wherever you go, your house is probably crawling with items that you thought you'd use more often, but simply haven't. Box them up and cart them away and begin the liberating process of de-cluttering.

2. *If you only use it once in a while, you can rent or share it.*

Maybe you've used a certain item recently, but you know you use it rarely. Chances are, you don't use a ladder, a pasta maker, or your shoe buffer all that often. But you do use it sometimes, so getting rid of it doesn't seem prudent. Unless you can buddy up. If your friend has the same items, approach her about working out an arrangement to share use when you need it. Let her know that you're selling or donating your circular saw, but you might need to use hers in a few months. Offer to even pay a small amount, or better yet, reciprocate the favor. If she needs an iron only once in a blue moon—and you iron religiously each Sunday—then it seems like a fair trade for everyone if she gets rid of her ironing board.

Take stock of the major tools and appliances in your home. What can you share? What can you rent? Make a list and then send an e-mail to your group of friends to see what everyone can collectively share. This was a skill you were taught in preschool; finally, it's coming in handy.

3.   *If it doesn't enhance your life, you should dump it.*

This rule applies to both household items and boyfriends. Your life will be much simpler and less stressful if you fill it only with things that add value and meaning. You want things (and people) that improve your life, not detract from it.

There are probably things you bought thinking they'd improve your life but have done anything but. They might not actually be hurting you, but they're clearly not helping. Fitness equipment usually falls into this category. You bought that fancy abdominal accessory but never quite got around to using it. Now it just sits there in the corner of your bedroom, ignored and alone. It's time for it to go.

Machines that promised to help you cook healthy food, and books and gadgets that you thought would save you time—these can all disappear, too, if they're not truly helping you achieve some goal. These items could be useful, but they're not useful to you. It's no fault of their own. Your life and your schedule just didn't allow you to take full advantage of them. Instead of idly wishing and hoping that you'll actually use them one day, make the tough decision and toss them out. They are adding no value.

As a side note, people can also be classified like this. There are people you know who add nothing to your life. In fact, they might take and take, never even thanking you. It's okay to dump them and spend time with others who appreciate you. It's easy to get rid of inanimate stuff when looking to de-clutter and simplify, but sometimes, people can cause just as much stress and distraction. Sift through them carefully, however; they're not a rice cooker to be boxed and taken to Goodwill.

4. *If several things can be replaced by one thing, get rid of them all.*

Modern technology continues to fascinate me. Following Moore's law, it seems that the capacity of our computers and phones doubles every eighteen months. That's right—if you go and buy a new laptop today, it will be only half as good as a new laptop will be in a year and a half. The world moves quickly.

Speaking of laptops, owning one could allow you to get rid of several items in your house. The beauty of a rapidly increasing technological world is that things get better. Remember when phones couldn't take pictures? When directions weren't spoken to you by a kind GPS voice? When the

Internet couldn't be accessed wirelessly from anywhere?

Likewise, more and more gadgets can all be replaced by one new one. So, if you get a new phone for a present that also plays music, you can get rid of that old MP3 player. Or, from a low-tech standpoint, if an emergency flashlight also comes with a radio, your old boom boxes can hit the road. Look around your house. If you have something that can do the job of three other somethings, then *voila!* You've just purged your life of three things you don't need.

In the 1880s soldiers needed a tool that would allow them to open canned food rations and repair their service rifle. There was no use in carrying two tools into battle if you could easily put everything you needed into one handy device. The result? The Swiss Army Knife.

5. *If you don't know you have it, you won't miss it.*

It happens to all of us: we're busy searching for a pair of scissors, and in the drawer we're rummaging through we find a necklace we forgot we owned. Or when looking for a hammer, we stumble upon a nice multi-tool we got for Christmas one year. Indeed, it can feel like Christmas all over again.

Although it's nice to find "new" things, this reality should be sobering. We own so much stuff that we can't even remember it all. The best thing about moving is the chance to find things you forgot you had (and to get rid of them). Be honest with yourself: if you forgot you even had it, would you miss it if it were gone? Probably not. So why not get rid of it? The next time you have a *eureka!* moment, quickly say good-bye to what it is you rediscover and place it in a sack to be donated the next time you're out.

6. *If you have more than one, donate the rest.*

Our lives and homes are full of duplicates. Think about it: How many winter coats do you own? Pairs of shoes? Rolls of wrapping paper? Dish sets, screwdrivers, or umbrellas? Somewhere along the way we became convinced that one wasn't enough. We needed more and more of the same thing.

Where should I donate my stuff?

If what you're getting rid of is still in good shape, it can be donated and put to good use somewhere else. Depending upon where you live, you should have your choice of salvage stores, nonprofit charities, or other places to donate your old stuff.

Before you take anything, it's always good to call ahead. Some places might not be accepting certain items any longer. And some places even offer at-home pickup of items. So, calling ahead could save you a trip.

It's also important to see whether you can meet a specific need. Perhaps someone at your place of worship needs a set of towels or some clothes; maybe a nonprofit organization needs your old furniture; it's possible a homeless shelter can use your dishes or other kitchen utensils. Being able to match your old stuff with an immediate, relevant need is a great feeling. So, ask around your inner circle to see where your items can be best used.

Granted, owning only one pair of shoes is a bit extreme, but so is owning thirty. I can't tell you what number is right for you, but I'm willing to bet that the number you currently have is too much. Paring down your collection of sweaters and board games could simplify your life instantly. You might not have the exact same sweater, but you do have sweaters in four different shades of blue. And although you don't own two identical copies of the same board game, the ones you rarely play can easily be given to someone who will appreciate them more.

Here's the drill: If you had to move somewhere half the size of your current home, what would you take? My wife and I recently moved out of our house while it was being renovated. Very quickly we had to decide which clothes and things we'd need for the next few months. Though tough, it was humbling and liberating to see how much we owned, and subsequently, how much we could do without. Upon moving back in, we rounded up many of our possessions and got rid of them.

Which sets of things that you own can be cut in half?

7. *If a digital version exists, purge your analog copy.*

There is no reason to keep something if you can find it online. Instruction manuals are the main culprit here. Even though you might think that keeping a set of assembly instructions for your bookcase is convenient, it's only taking up precious room on said bookcase. If you need to take it apart, I'm sure you can find how to do so on the Internet.

You can also find phone directories online. And music. And photographs. There are even services that will digitize all of your documents, if you want to go to that extreme and not own any paper anymore (not a bad idea). Our digital world keeps getting better and storage keeps getting cheaper; the downside and risks to storing digitally are rapidly disappearing. If you know you can access it online, there's no reason to keep it around offline.

8. *If you've already upgraded, don't hang on to the previous edition.*

In college, I always tried to buy my textbooks used. I would save a fortune doing so, and if I were going to use it for only a semester, I didn't care what was highlighted or how tattered the cover was. What irked me, however, was when a new edition came out, rendering all previous copies obsolete. There is no such thing as a used new textbook.

The same is true of everything else that can be upgraded. When you have the latest version, there's no reason to hang on to the older one. When you get a new phone, be sure to unload the old one. If you receive a new camera as a gift, sell your old one if it still works well. Books, computers, cars, and TVs—when the new has come, let the old one go. The upside—in addition to clearing out clutter—is that in most cases, you can sell your previous versions and earn a little cash. Assuming your old video camera, stereo receiver, and iPod are in good condition, you'll actually make money by simplifying your life.

9. *If it generates negative energy, you don't need it or its vibes.*

We've already discussed needing to get rid of something if it's not proactively improving your life, but if it is actually creating negative thoughts or feelings, it needs to go. Immediately.

A friend of mine is a decorating consultant, and she was telling me about one of her clients. In helping create a living space that was warm and inviting, she discovered that her client owned a vase she just couldn't seem to put in the right place. With each arrangement, the client seemed more and more frustrated. Finally, my friend asked the client where the vase came from. As it turned out, a relative had given her the vase and the two were no longer on good terms. As such, no matter where the vase went, looking at it resulted in negative and angry feelings. My friend wisely asked if the vase could be given away. The client obliged, and the space instantly felt more personal and nearly perfect.

What do you own that produces negative thoughts when you see it? Whatever it is, it needs to go. Whether it's a vase someone gave you, a piece of art, or an ugly couch, if it makes you angry, get rid of it. Keeping this item around will only add stress and anger to your life, and you don't need either. The next time you feel something you own is upsetting you, move it to the donate pile. Don't let the thing you own end up owning you.

10. *If you don't want it, then you shouldn't keep it.*

Remember: of everything you own, you get to decide the terms of ownership. If you don't want it anymore, sell it or give it away. It's yours to do with as you please. If you don't want it, don't keep it.

This seems easier said than done. No matter what it is, you might feel a sense of guilt or obligation when you try to get rid of something. Perhaps you're reminded of how much you paid for something. Getting rid of it, then, can feel like such a waste. But should it? Let's say you paid $100 for a jacket that you now rarely wear. You own four other jackets, so this one can easily go. Let's pretend that in its heyday, you wore that jacket 200 times. That means you paid $0.50 to wear that jacket each time. That seems like a modest price to stay warm and look great. Your money wasn't wasted, then. You got a great deal!

Just because something can last forever doesn't mean that it should. Sometimes, we do make boneheaded purchasing decisions, but this is part of life. Even if the purchase was immature or regrettable, we can reclaim and make up for that mistake by wisely getting rid of things we don't need. Lose the trumped-up sense of obligation and decide what it is you really want in life. Keep those things and get rid of everything else. You'll be happier and clutter-free by doing so.

Even though many others will try to convince you otherwise, it really is all about you. You have one life. Do something.

Set up a brain trust

As you seek to simplify your life and turn your dreams into reality, you'll need help in the form of feedback. If life is about process and progress, you need a group of peers who understands you and can keep you on track. If you want to keep out clutter—especially the clutter that ideas and impulses can quickly create—then you need a small group of people to help you stay focused.

I call this group a "brain trust" and have used them time and again to tell whether an idea is a good one. I also draw on them for support and encouragement when needed. The brain trust can also provide a certain level of accountability as they check in with you to see how you're progressing toward your personal goals.

Here's what a brain trust does and how to set one up.

- *Find at least two other people.* Pick some folks you know and admire for their ability to think. Maybe they look at problems from a fresh angle. Maybe they're creative. Maybe they aren't afraid to ask "Why?" Regardless, pinpoint at least two other people you know you can learn from.

- *Find a third place.* Even if you choose to meet with coworkers, get out of the office. Or if you meet with roommates or family, get out of the house. Go to a place meant for conversation, like a coffee shop, restaurant, park, or bar. This neutral ground will force you to stay engaged instead of worried about someone needing the conference room.

- *Come with a question.* Take turns each bringing a question to the others. One week someone might ask, "How can we set up a group that brings about community change the best?" Or, "What is our city's biggest need?" The conversation might drift from that, but with a central question to get you started, your group can begin with a reference point.

- *Let it happen.* Other than the question, there should be no set agenda. There's no format, no talking stick, no rules. Allowing the conversation to go where it may means you can answer the question from your perspective, bringing your unique approach. You might end up 180 degrees from where you started, but that's the beauty of the meeting.

Whether you're dreaming about social ills or a way to improve air travel, forming a brain trust with other smart people means that the next big thing could happen during the next regularly scheduled coffee hour.

When should you meet?

My brain trust tries our best to meet regularly, roughly every two weeks. Because each of our schedules varies widely, we need to stay flexible. We enjoy meeting in person at a local coffee shop over breakfast. This allows for more personal, face-to-face time to pick each other's brains and to really let the ideas fly. Dropping an idea in front of this group is eerily nerve-wracking. When you say something among them, you're literally putting your best self out there. Sharing an idea for a project, business, or personal goal requires vulnerability. But your brain trust is made up of trusting peers, so even if your idea is a terrible one, everyone remains friends.

You could decide to meet digitally, too. I have another group of people who don't live in Nashville that I e-mail when faced with big decisions. I welcome each of their feedback and seek their input roughly twice a year. They are friends I've accumulated over the years whom I admire for what they do for a living, the kind of lives they lead, and the kind of people they're becoming.

The digital and physical aspects of a brain trust should not be overlooked; each has its own merits and benefits, and you—like me—might benefit from using both. When meeting in person, you won't need to get together more than once a week.

Sometimes, you might need to call a special session if something arises unexpectedly. Again, let each member know why you need to meet so they can be thinking of ideas or solutions to help. Like all meetings, set a beginning and ending time so people can best plan their schedules.

Find a mentor

If a brain trust is a peer group of equals that can provide feedback and encouragement, a mentor is a single superior who can do the same thing. In order to simplify your life and stay on track to accomplishing your biggest and best dreams, your life needs a mentor.

A mentor is different than a hero or an idol. A mentor personally knows you. A mentor can offer advice and direction based on your lot in life because they know who you are. You could e-mail Rafael Nadal for advice on tennis or Tina Fey for questions about writing, and their advice might be sound and inspirational (if they answer you). But it won't take into account that you have a family, must live in a certain place, or face unique personal obstacles. A mentor's advice, on the other hand, will always be relevant because it's personal.

Mentors can also guide you for a certain period of life. Because they know you, they can offer input to get you where you want to go for the next five years, or while you're working in a certain career field. They might not be able to offer advice for an extended period of time, but what they can offer is relevant immediately, and this is a great thing.

Therefore, in order to find a mentor, take stock of where you are in life right now. Look around you; is there a boss or professor who could play a mentoring role? Is there a wise pastor or an insightful leader in your life who could take you under his or her wing once you've articulated what it is you're trying to become? If so, your immediate personal circle is a great place to look to find a mentor.

In order to easily find and work with a mentor, follow these three steps:

1.   Clue them in.

When you've identified someone who can serve as a mentor, let them know you'd like them to do so. They'll provide better advice and encouragement if they know they're playing this role in your life.

2.   Be specific.

Let them know why you'd like them to mentor you. What have they accomplished that you'd like to achieve? What is it about them that can better develop what you're trying to become? Why are they uniquely positioned to offer you the best insight and advice during this season of life?

3.   Tell them where you want to go.

So that they can begin to offer timely input, share with them your dreams, passions, plans, and actions. Tell them about the work you're doing now in order to get where you'd like to go. Showing that you're willing to do the hard work to improve your life will prove that you're serious about developing something important and meaningful. It will also help them see your progress so they can offer the best advice at the right time.

If you're wondering what this looks like, here's a short letter that encapsulates all three of the above steps. Copy and paste this into an e-mail if you like, and best of luck landing a mentor who will help you conquer your dreams!

Dear Dr. Felton:

I'm writing today to ask if you would be willing to be my mentor. I feel like this is a crucial time in my life; I believe the next five years—if done right—will set me on the course to living my dream life. I'm seeking you out as a mentor because I see you as someone who works in a field I'd love to be a part of; you also seem to have achieved so much with circumstances similar to mine.

I'm not asking you to casually offer advice, but rather to help me make sure I'm on the right track. I recently completed my Personal Strategic Plan, a time of intense work and reflection that clearly articulates the steps I need to take to achieve the biggest goals I have for myself. I'm happy to treat you to coffee to show you this and to discuss how we might work together.

Thanks for your time. I still remember how you pushed me hard to think more critically in your class last year. That skill has come in handy many times already.

Sincerely,

Sam

Should you have a hero?

A hero is different than a mentor because a hero doesn't know you. A hero is someone you admire from afar because they have a very specific skill you'd like to have. Usually, they are famous, like entertainers or athletes.

It's okay (and even recommended) to have a hero, but never mistake them for a mentor. A hero has a seemingly supernatural ability in a particular area, and that's why you admire them. A hero is someone like Abraham Lincoln, Paul McCartney, Oprah Winfrey, or Carrie Underwood.

A hero is great to have because he or she reminds you of how great you can be. You have an ultimate standard to shoot for. But be careful not to idolize a hero in every area of life. I'd love to play golf like Tiger Woods, but I'd never look to him for advice on how to be a great husband.

Be mindful, then, that you can drop a hero at any time. Should you appreciate someone's particular ability and then they do something that seems un-hero-like, simply move on to someone else. Because you have no personal connection, it's easy to change heroes at your convenience.

7

de-stressing in order
to be happier

7

de-stressing
in order to be happier

Why stress is so stressful

In 1983, *Time* magazine ran a cover story declaring that stress was America's leading health problem. *Prevention* published a survey thirteen years later showing that 75 percent of us feel "great stress" at least once a week. Things don't seem to be improving much, either. The world is moving faster than ever. Deadlines, bills, recessions, changes—they all combine to make every one of us more stressed, more on edge, and more at risk for deeper sicknesses than ever before. To date, the *New England Journal of Medicine* has published over 1,000 articles or studies about stress. Clearly, we're facing a major problem.

Stress refers to the failure of someone to respond appropriately when threatened. If a deadline on a big project looms and you're curled in fetal position on the bathroom floor instead of fine-tuning your presentation, it's safe to say that you're stressed. Stress can cause a host of other problems, too, like hypertension, strokes, diabetes, ulcers, and back pain.

Stress is ultimately caused, of course, by a stressor. A stressor is usually an external factor. Such examples can happen on a daily basis, like traffic jams, long lines, misplacing your keys, or financial strains. Stressors can also be major life changes like moving, divorce, or deaths of relatives. In addition, stressors can happen in the workplace, like having a boss who's always on your case, being frustrated with your role or how much you make, or even disliking the number and type of meetings you're required to attend. In fact, the American Institute of Stress (yes, there is such a thing) estimates that as many as 80 percent of all workers are stressed, and that stress collectively costs companies upwards of $300 billion a year.

It seems logical then, than in order to de-stress your life, you simply need to remove the stressor, the thing that's causing all of your stress. Remove the cause and you'll eliminate the effect.

This is most easily done when the stressor is an object or an everyday situation. If you hate sitting in traffic, telecommute or find an alternate route. If being able to afford everything stresses you out, embrace a lifestyle of spending less. And if watching your team lose every week makes you feel depressed, turn off the TV and don't watch the games (or read the recap on the sports page).

But what about when your job causes you stress? The crisis of work as discussed in chapter three can certainly be seen as a stressor. Indeed, it's designed to elicit a response—to put you in a place where you come face-to-face with your impending reality and decide whether you want to change it all. But should you completely remove work from your life if it causes you stress? Or should you seek to find work that aligns with the values and strengths you discovered while penning your Personal Strategic Plan?

Unless you're independently wealthy or live an incredibly frugal lifestyle, you'll need to work. But it doesn't have to cause you stress. In fact, work can even be a relief, if approached from the right perspective. The rest of this chapter will focus on ideas to help you de-stress your life by finding work you love.

When should you quit your job?

Unless you are willing to risk it all to create a crisis moment in your current line of work and walk out the door, don't quit your job after you finish reading this book. My line of work allows me to meet and talk with many young people—college students or recent graduates—who want to leave their current job and set out on their own. Although they may be ambitious dreamers, they're actually just facing the crisis of work for the first time, staring the next forty years in the face and wondering what to do.

Usually, somewhere in the conversation, they say, "I'm thinking about quitting my job in order to go do _____." Then they fill in the blank with what might be a great idea but could actually be nothing more than a casual interest, definitely not something they should build a career around.

I tell each of them, "Don't quit your job. No matter how much you hate it, don't quit until you literally can't take it anymore. Keep working where you are until you think you're going to harm yourself or someone else. Then—and only then—walk out."

This might seem like contradictory advice from the guy who quit his job on the fly simply because he couldn't take working in a job that didn't use his passions or talents. But I know that unemployment (or underemployment) can also cause stress. Without knowing where you're going, you're better off staying put.

If, however, you've done your Dream to Action Plan and your Personal Strategic Plan, and the next best step is to leave where you are and set out on your own, so be it. After you complete each plan, you'll have a clear sense of direction and know what it is you need to do. Don't quit on a whim unless you can't take it another day. Leaving your current position to take a job more to your liking or to follow your clearly articulated dreams and passions is a much wiser step, one that has much less regret and second guessing, each of which can cause stress in their own right.

But even when you've defined who you want to be and how you need to become that person, quitting your job still might not be in the cards. You can easily test out a business idea or a new line of work by staying employed forty hours a week. It will take some sacrifice, but it's possible. How? Just find an extra hour in each day. Stop watching *CSI*. Wake up early or stay up late. Take shorter lunch breaks. Ask your boss if you can work four ten-hour days instead of five eight-hour ones, and use the extra day to chase down your passion. An extra hour a day for a year amounts to more than forty-five eight-hour workdays of time. And all you had to do was change your TV habit.

Ultimately, you need to best navigate risk. Tolerance of risk is different for everyone; my wife and I are polar opposites when it comes to taking risks. Roller coasters and starting companies aren't for everyone.

Should you start your own company?

Starting and running my own business has been one of the hardest things I've ever done. I never received any formal business training, so that could be part of the problem. But spending the time, money, and energy required to grow a successful company has shown me that the entrepreneurial path isn't for everyone.

Sure, anyone can start a company. But not everyone can grow and manage one. Starting a company only requires a trip to the courthouse to fill out some papers. But making that company successful is an entirely different endeavor. Just because you hate your job doesn't mean you need to set out on your own. If you're wondering whether owning a business is right for you, ask yourself these questions:

How much risk can I tolerate?

Starting a business isn't easy or automatic. It requires effort, deliberate action, and financial risk. The good thing is that there can be financial reward if all goes well. But taking on the burden of starting a company also means that your name, credit, and even some other assets are on the line. Are you willing to risk that? What would you be willing to lose if it didn't work out? How much money would it be worth if you failed and were merely left with a great learning experience?

How you answer this question will help you know whether you should start your own business and what kind of business it should be. Some opportunities will require less up-front money than others; some companies can be started only with a lot of investment capital and a very detailed business plan. If you're not the risk-taking type, then you can try out your business idea as a hobby, making money as you can on the side. Once you've developed a customer base, you can look at scaling things up and growing, doing so with a bit less risk since you've already proven there's a market for what you're offering. The risk never really disappears, but it can be wisely navigated.

Is there really an opportunity here?

A professor of entrepreneurship and I were having coffee, and he let me in on the best advice he gives students and those looking to start a new business. He said that he reminds them: "There may be a gap in the market, but is there a market in the gap?" In other words, just because you think there is a need for a product or service you can offer, does it mean that enough people will line up to pay you for it?

For example, there's no such thing as a vacuum cleaner that doubles as a microwave. You might conclude, then, there is a gap in the market. You could fill in this gap by buying a factory and mass producing the world's first Vacuum-Wave 3000. But before you do, it will pay to do some more research into this. Would people really want a device that both cleans the carpet and cooks your food? I don't even know how this gadget would work, but just because it doesn't exist doesn't mean that it should. Be careful before launching something. Do your homework and make sure there is a demonstrated need for what you want to offer the world.

How well do I know this industry?

The companies I started are in industries I know something about, namely, writing and marketing. I would never start a health-care company, a record label, or a coffee shop. Each could be fun, fulfilling, and financially viable, but I would have a very difficult go of it seeing as how I know very little about these three worlds.

If you see an opportunity before you, make sure it plays to one of your ten strengths you listed in your Personal Strategic Plan. Better yet, make sure it capitalizes on a strength and uses a core passion of yours from your Dream to Action Plan. Do what you know. If you want to do something else, learn about it first. Then you can see whether it makes sense to take the risk and launch a company in that sector. The most successful entrepreneurs are those who create opportunities in areas they know well.

How will I know when it's time to quit?

This might seem like a rather odd and depressing question. Wouldn't it be more uplifting to ask when you'll know that you're successful? Not necessarily. Success is easy to recognize when you own your own business: the doors are still open. You're making money, finding new customers, and staying busy. Product is moving off the shelves, new orders are coming in, and you're hiring more employees. Success is easy to pinpoint.

Failure, on the other hand, can exist for years before you realize it. You can tread water and hemorrhage money and time for quite a while before it dawns on you that you should have quit years earlier. This is why goal-setting is key. This is why the plan and action portions of your Dream to Action Plan have a lot of questions about measurement. You need to know when you're not succeeding so you can cut your losses and move on. You'll de-stress your life and business when you make the right decision to shut it down and move on to something more viable. Set targets in appropriate areas and tell yourself that if you don't hit three of those within a certain time-frame, it's time to close your doors and move on to something that has a better chance of success.

Remember: even if you become your own boss, there are no guarantees that work will no longer cause you stress. In fact, some of the most stressed-out people I know are entrepreneurs. The pursuit of a financial windfall or even just financial stability causes them to work long hours and see their family even less than if they were to work for a large corporation. In other words, their lives could be simpler if they worked a job they hated instead of one they loved. It sounds counterintuitive (and even foreboding), but starting your own company is no golden ticket on the Stress-Free Express. You'll still need to say yes to the right opportunities and make sure you have the right stuff—and not the wrong stuff—in your life. For me, that means I find a partner to share the responsibility—and the success—with.

Find a partner

I don't believe in doing things alone. Whether you decide to start your own company or look for a new job, you're better off doing so with someone else. The right partner can provide inspiration, motivation, and education. No matter what you're creating—whether a business or a baby—you're better off doing it with someone else.

I've started two companies now, each with a co-founder. In all my years of running each company, I've never minded typing "co" in front of the word "founder." Doing so actually gives me a sense of pride, the same sense you might think would come only with going at something alone and soaking in all the credit that comes with blazing a trail.

The truth is that no one does something entirely by himself or herself. There are no true solo acts. Even if the equity or accolades aren't shared, there is always someone behind the scenes. Whether it's a supportive spouse, helpful parents, a team of experts, or the wisdom of those who have gone before you, there is comfort and confidence in knowing that you're not alone in what you do.

A partner is good to have because they share the burden with you. Although moral and emotional support is nice to have, a partner is willing to take a risk with you. They're willing to stick their neck out as you stick yours out. Their name is on the line and their skin is in the game. They—like you—are all in. They're betting big and playing to win. You're not the only one with your cards on the table. They're taking a shot, too.

It's best to have a partner who complements you and doesn't mirror you. Finding someone with a different yet complementary skill set is invaluable. Ideally, each of you will do at least one thing better than the other. In a best-case scenario, everything your business or project needs to do can be done by both of you working together. Your fate, then, rises and falls with one another.

This, again, is why completing the two major tools in this book—the Dream to Action Plan and your Personal Strategic Plan—is crucial. If done right, each will help you meet the right people, whether they serve as a support network or official business partners.

Can't I just play golf?

Outside of the working world, one way to eliminate stress is to do something relaxing. Some people relax by playing golf, some do yoga, others go for a jog, some watch TV to unwind, and others get lost in a good book. These temporary distractions that often take the form of a hobby can be simple ways to escape the daily grind of a stressful job.

But take caution: you must be very careful to not let a hobby or leisurely pursuit cause the very stress it should be counteracting. Many people I know claim that playing golf or going fishing calms or de-stresses them—until they try to hit it out of the sand trap or reel in their big catch. Then, they're cussing and fighting and stressing so much you might think they're at work.

Hobbies—like jobs—must be tried on a few times before finding the right fit. It's okay to hop from one thing to another looking for a regular activity that truly calms you and resets your internal stress meter. The minute you feel obligated or guilty about a hobby, however, is the minute it can actually begin to *add* stress to your life.

I like reading books; it's a way for me to be consumed with a singular activity and let other worries fade into the background for a few hours. I used to make sure I finished any book I started—even bad ones. Soon enough, the feeling of obligation became too much and began to make reading less enjoyable. I immediately gave myself permission to not finish a book if I didn't like it. The stress was lifted, and reading once again became a fun way to spend time and put my mind at ease.

Finding a distraction for your stress is a good way to counteract its potentially negative effects. Even though you'll be adding an activity to your life, the benefits you gain by taking time to care for yourself and enjoy what you're doing—even for a small amount of time—will be well worth it.

For me, I've found that to truly fight the stress in my life, an activity must consistently take my mind off the stressor. The activity I'm enjoying must transport me somewhere else, where I don't think about impending deadlines or other obligations. My hobbies and leisurely pursuits help me to relax by allowing me to focus only on the enjoyable task at hand. I'm not truly relaxing if my mind wanders to work.

This is why I don't use TV to combat stress. Sitting in a recliner and only moving my thumb might look relaxing, but my mind is still racing. I need something—like reading, running, or golfing—that takes my mind off the stressors and demands in life and focuses deliberately on something I enjoy.

Try as many hobbies as you like. Learn to play croquet. Take up knitting. Join your local kite-flying club. Find something that puts your mind at ease and makes you feel as stress free as possible.

Removing clutter and what causes us stress—which is usually work related—will ultimately make us happier, if we can keep everything in balance. That's how we know we have arrived after all that time spent planning and processing. When we feel as though we have a very healthy, active, and recognizable balance in our lives, things are finally simple enough.

What about "good" stress?

Not all stress has to be bad. Some stressors can actually cause us to perform better. There are moments when all of us—not just star athletes—are clutch, coming through when the stakes are highest. Of course, it's up for debate whether it's the pressure-packed situation that causes us to meet the challenge, or the time spent in practice and study that's helping us through.

Star baseball players always seem to get the big hit in the bottom of the ninth inning because they've spent most of their lives hitting a baseball. If I were to walk up to the plate, even if I perform well when speaking to a large crowd, I would fare much more poorly than they would against a 90 mph fastball. I wouldn't be prepared.

And that's the thing about "good" stress. The stress of any given situation is lessened by being prepared for such a high-impact moment. The simple solution? Spend less time worrying about the big game (or meeting or presentation or date) and more time preparing for it. Use the free time you gain by doing what truly matters to get ready for your big moment in the spotlight.

8

staying balanced

8

staying balanced

If simplicity is about getting more of the right stuff and less of the wrong stuff in your life, then it's really all about balance. It's about keeping things in check and manageable. It's about living your life and organizing it in such a way that you can move as you wish. Simplicity means you can take advantage of the right opportunities when they arise. It means you're not bogged down and burdened by so much stuff. It means that you have all of what you need and a lot of what you want. You've got just the right amount of everything so you can live the life you've always imagined.

I think we misunderstand balance, however. We automatically think that balance means having everything in equal parts. This is not our fault; the timeless image of a scale makes us think that one side has to be equal to the other side. So, if we are to achieve "work-life balance" (which many experts suggest will make us happy), we need to have equal amounts of work and life. Spend eight hours at work and then eight hours at life (and then eight hours at sleeping so we can go back and repeat the balanced cycle). I think this is a misguided notion of balance. Balance does not mean equality.

Life is not lived standing still. Rarely do we have time to pause and weigh what we're spending time doing. Besides, none of us thinks in terms of work-life balance, calculating each minute we spend working or living in order to make sure we have equal parts of each before we go to bed.

I hate this term, too, because I think it's in the wrong order. It makes it sound like work is more important than life. Of course, work is part of life, unable to be separated. When discussing this topic, I prefer to use the term life-work balance. Since life is more important than what we do to earn money, I want to make sure I'm filling that life with as much stuff that matters, including what I do to earn a paycheck.

I prefer to think about balance not in terms of a scale where one side always equals another, but rather in terms of a balance beam. A gymnast on a beam is a much more dynamic image. She's moving. There is action. She is accelerating at times, pausing at others, and somehow, managing to flip and fly and make it all work on a four-inch-wide bar.

When you watch closely, it's amazing how anyone is able to stay balanced. Many gymnasts look wobbly at times, just like we do when trying to manage all the requirements and obligations in our lives. A gymnast on a beam doesn't look anything like a scale, though both can be perfectly balanced. A scale is symmetrical and equal; a gymnast is contorted and seemingly all over the place. She sticks out a leg in one direction to balance an entire torso headed in the opposite direction. She leaves her feet and when she lands, her arms instinctively jut right and left, up and down to keep her on the beam as she moves forward.

Motion. That's the difference between a balance beam and scales. Progress. Momentum. We're always trying to balance—between life and work, home and the office, friends and family, debt and earnings, passion and dreams, plans and actions, hopes and reality. And we're doing so while going to work, being parents, helping others, saving for tomorrow, and trying to make time for ourselves.

We need to stay balanced in life and in work not so we can have all things in equal measure, like our hypothetical scales. We stay balanced so we can stay up on the beam, where the action is. We need balance in our lives—the balance that comes through simplicity—in order to keep going, to keep tumbling and flipping and walking and running. Life is always in motion, and if we want to keep up, we need to figure out how to stay balanced.

Now that you're at the end of the book, I hope you've found a way to do just that. Getting rid of the clutter and stress that your life doesn't need will certainly make you happier. It will also keep things simpler, which will keep you balanced as you jump and flip through life. And that's the key. That's why we want to keep things simple—so we can stay on the beam. You have one life, one shot out there on that beam.

Do something.